REMINDERS FOR LIFE

DAILY INSPIRATIONAL MESSAGES THAT UPLIFT, ENCOURAGE, AND HELP DEVELOP A MINDSET FOR CREATING LASTING HAPPINESS

BY COMMANDING LIFE

Reminders for Life
Daily Inspirational Messages that Uplift, Encourage, and Help Develop a Mindset for Creating Lasting Happiness

Cover photo by Sandra Seitamaa via Unsplash

www.CommandingLife.com

ISBN 978-1-7325400-9-5

January 01

I am already receiving more blessings.

This year will be amazing for me. Obstacles will be removed. I will be redirected to more. Bigger bridges will be built to better. Abundance will appear all around me. Support will show up right on time. Divine connections will be made. Clarity will resolve all concerns. Love will prevail. Miracles will manifest. Happiness will happen. I am ready for all good things to flow to me. I am already loved. I am already abundant. I am already at peace. I am already happy. I am already fulfilled. I am already successful. I am already observing unlimited possibilities. I am already receiving. I am already blessed. I am already whole. I am already thriving. I am ALL READY.

January 02

I am always in a season of abundance.

What you want always shows up when you are ready. When you ask for blessings, you must be willing to figure out where the work must be done to prepare for them. Your readiness could be changed mindset, improved habits, or commitment to consistent action. Whatever you are praying for, create it in your life, and more will manifest. If you are praying for prosperity, try planting and preparing for a harvest. If you are praying for the hurt to go away, practice healing with self-care. If you are praying for unconditional love, start with self-compassion. If you are praying for more support, believe in who you are. Consider your requests delivered. Remember, you already have what it takes to create your all.

January 03

I am destined for great things.

Temporary challenges help you develop permanent improvements with who you are and what you can produce for your life. Everything you don't want is showing you how to create what you do want. Your experiences are designed to level you up to more. Whatever you think is blocking, delaying, or distracting you, is only directing you to the life you desire. Today pay attention to the blessings showing up for you and find what you need to reenergize your journey. Empower your well-being by setting boundaries that define what you deserve to have within your life. Celebrate your progress by remembering why you started. Keep going and trust you are destined for a life more significant than you can currently perceive.

January 04

I am aware of my true worth.

You can change what you perceive as possible when you improve the thoughts that prevent you from living your full potential. Recognizing your true worth is about transforming your life beyond the learned limits that created a lack mindset. Expand your perspective by gaining control of what you can create. Start by acknowledging that a belief is only a thought you continue to think. Remember, you can always amend beliefs that do not serve your thriving. You have what it takes to redefine how valuable you identify your life to be. Believe in the abundant possibilities for your future and expect they will manifest. The moment you start imagining you are capable of creating more, you will welcome more. You are worthy of all good things.

January 05

I am clear about my desires.

You don't have to be whole to be lovable. You don't have to be fully healed to understand happiness. You don't have to possess anything to welcome abundance. You don't have to be passive to live in peace. You don't have to be lacking before you figure out you deserve more. You don't have to overcome fear to choose faith. Whatever you desire does not require perfection before it can manifest. Everything you can imagine possible is already available and ready to be realized. It is up to you to decide what you want and make the mental and emotional room to receive it. Exercise your power of choice in the thoughts, beliefs, and responses you generate. Remember, you are a powerful creator born to create. It is your birthright to build the life you desire.

January 06

I am pursuing what makes me happy.

When you choose to heal, you begin the process of advocating for your mental, emotional, and spiritual well-being. Healing is about leaving the effects of the past behind and redirecting your focus to what is needed to thrive in the present. It is your daily choice to intentionally live in the moment. Make the change by pursuing what makes you feel your best. Support your journey by consistently practicing positive emotions like gratitude. You feel blessed when you acknowledge who you are and what you are capable of creating. You feel hopeful when you trust things will work out for you. You feel whole when you accept you already have everything you need to blossom. Every day make your well-being a priority.

January 07

I am ready to step into the sunshine.

You may occasionally get impatient or develop disbelief in the possibility of your dreams, but it is at these moments you learn to thrive. When you feel like giving up, choose to rest and recharge rather than quit on your happiness. Struggle does not mean you should stop; it is an indication that something must be improved before you move forward. Every experience helps you choose what you create next. Remember, you are constantly defining what you want versus what you don't want. The journey will continuously change; trust you have what it takes to advance. Stay motivated by appreciating and celebrating your progress. It will all be worth it every time you overcome and step into the sunshine.

January 08

I am a magnet for abundance.

You consistently produce your prosperity from the experiences that show you how to discern and develop bigger dreams. What you go through is helping you define more of what you want to welcome. Today focus on the blessings already surrounding you. Gratitude for the abundance of goodness in the simple things will create more. Remember, you are the point of attraction, and your desires will flow to you. Be open to your prosperity being received in multiple ways and at various times. What is for you will never miss you, have faith in that. Trust that all is well and move forward with a renewed sense of hope and assurance. You have asked for more, believe it will manifest for you soon. A blessing that has started will always be completed.

January 09

I am welcoming my thriving.

People sometimes chase what they think is best without considering what they need to feel happy and satisfied. Many are focused on future happiness, not understanding that the only way to be contented with their life is to embrace the present. Fulfillment is about finding what you need to flourish in the now, then using that to create the life you want. The next time your mind wanders into an uncertain future, refocus on what is working in the present. Don't stay stuck surviving because you are constantly deferring your happiness to when. Thrive by making the daily decision to find something to appreciate despite the circumstances. Take the time to discover who you are, and your deepest desires will be easier to materialize. The joy you seek is unfolding right now.

January 10

I am mastering what I need to pursue my joy.

The only way to be happy is to feel happy. If you are always looking for joy in people, places, and things, you might eventually get disappointed when they don't deliver. Remember, happiness is an emotion that is felt and can only be created by you. Instead of looking for joy outside of yourself, find what you need to experience it within. Work on feeling the same regardless of the location, destination, or situation. Making time to discover who you are and what brings you happiness will prepare you for any changes in your circumstances. Start with exploring what fills you up and energizes you. Concentrating on how you want to feel is not selfish; it is self-first.

January 11

I am hopeful and I will be abundant.

Get comfortable with the word 'wait.' Understand that a delay is never a denial of what you desire. Focus on what needs to be done before you get your 'yes.' Push past your fear and find your faith in the process. Sometimes, you are slowed down to learn how to master creating more. Life is always trying to steer you toward everything you asked for. Embrace today's opportunities to pursue the most significant life vision you can perceive. Yes, 'hold' can make you feel helpless. Instead, get hopeful for a bigger harvest. Remember, only your beliefs have limits; you are destined for a life full of abundant possibilities. Trust blessings will manifest for you daily. Get ready to receive your yes!

January 12

I am always given what I need to thrive.

You are never given a seed to plant without the provisions needed to grow it into the life you want. Don't delay the manifestation with doubt in what you deserve. Get grateful; you have been supported, provided for, and protected from circumstances you couldn't even imagine. Never lose hope when you cannot see a way, instead have faith that paths will be cleared ahead of you. When you think you are left to do it all alone, the Universe will show you it was silently preparing more than you can imagine. Focus on the good that is present and believe more will show up. Remember, keep the faith, big things can happen in short timeframes. You are always given what you need to thrive.

January 13

I am growing my small into my all.

Growth is never easy. Sometimes you need to fall before you rise, fail before you succeed, lose before you gain, and pause before you move forward. Credit yourself for the strength you found to keep going when you were unexpectedly pushed from your comfort zones. Do not disregard the significance of these experiences; they are helping you release the habits that do not serve your elevation to higher. Challenging times produce your desire to create more. What you don't want shows you how to identify what you do want. With time and nurturing, a little extra effort can grow into an extraordinary life. Everything small has the potential to become your all.

January 14

I am deserving of all that I desire.

You are deserving of all you can imagine. Be compassionate with yourself as you focus on the life you want to create. Start caring about what you say, it can help improve how you feel. You are the closest to your ear; pay attention to what you whisper about yourself. Remember, the loudest, most important voice is your own. Always use encouraging, loving, and uplifting words. Acknowledge you are capable of creating all of your dreams. Use what you have been through to push your way through. Confidently be your cheerleader; you are amazing. Remember, when you pray for blessings, you will always be given the Divine support to accomplish them. Love, abundance, and success are already within you, expanding and waiting to be unleashed.

January 15

I am improving daily.

Everyone has a chapter they are trying to forget. Facing your shadow can be scary, but it is necessary if you desire to be more intentional about creating your future. The past struggle developed the lasting skills needed to create abundance. The rejection improved your focus on self-love and self-worth. Remember, temporary challenges teach lifelong lessons. Use what you have gone through to create the future you want. Praising your progress will help you feel empowered as you move along your journey. Releasing the pressure to live a perfect life will bring permanent peace. Every day find a way to spotlight your positive attributes and you will discover more of your potential. Experiences may not last forever, but the knowledge gained will. You will prosper.

January 16

I am finding balance and harmony in my life.

Yes, negative emotions can occasionally consume your happiness, but you can offset them by being more mindful. Instead of overthinking about the future, regain your peace by doing what you enjoy in the present. Instead of battling your fears, build your faith and trust things are working out for you. Instead of focusing on lack, uplift yourself with gratitude for what you have already received. Instead of feeling disconnected, celebrate the loving relationships that surround you. You determine the emotional balance you create through every positive choice you make. Optimism is the best approach to overcoming any struggle. Remember, only you can take charge of how you want to feel daily.

January 17

I am leveling up to more.

When you ask for more, release the need to control how it should unfold. What you want is always coming to you through ways that encourage you to grow up, glow up, or get up. You grow up when you overcome the experiences that made you ask for more. You will glow up when you understand your true worth. You will get up to higher levels when you release the mindset that keeps you back. Life is always trying to level you up to what you asked for. The ease of this transition depends on your resistance to the process of change. Remember, who you were when you asked, is never the same person that receives the blessing. Believe that the transformation is for your highest good. Everything is working out for you. Trust the process that brings your desires.

January 18

I am response-ABLE.

You don't need someone to change before you find peace. You don't need to be successful before you feel abundant. You don't need the love of another before you begin to love yourself. Yes, it is easier to deflect blame, but your happiness is your responsibility. You cannot lead your life when you keep pushing yourself to the back. Give yourself designated well-being time every day. It is your responsibility to prioritize your happiness by being self-first enough to care about how you feel. Positive emotions and focused thoughts help you create the life you desire. The moment you understand you are response-ABLE, you begin to take charge of how you feel and the choices you make. You are the only one in control of your change. Start with being deliberate with your decisions.

January 19

I am self-first and self-compassionate.

You may not be able to control the actions of others, but you can remain at peace through your response to them. Remember, you have done the work to become a better version of yourself; take control by defining how others relate to you. You have the power to manage whether someone pulls you down to their level or if you stay elevated where you are. Keep setting boundaries, releasing the need for validation, removing self-imposed limits, leveling up, and reaping the rewards. Celebrate the great job you are doing to become the best version of yourself. Be proud of all your progress. Don't get distracted by things that have nothing to do with your goals. Self-first is not selfish.

January 20

I am patient with the process.

Your strength is built from every challenge you overcame. Your abundance is cultivated from every seed you have ever planted. Your peace is gained from every moment you sit still and embrace your faith. Your clarity is created in every moment you focus on your happiness. Every time you wish for more, make it your responsibility to prepare emotionally, spiritually, and mentally for it to happen. Start with trusting your request will manifest right on time. Be patient with the process that produces what you want. Do the inner work to build a better outer world. Then relax as you allow things to work out for you. What is yours will never miss you because you cannot mess up your destiny. Believe your blessings are already materializing.

January 21

I am doing the best I can.

Emotions like disappointment and exhaustion are temporary experiences that you can use to work in your favor. They are natural states that you go through to get to the breakthrough. Everyone deals with their emotions differently; some people move through theirs faster than others. Never be ashamed of your pace. Use the moon to remind you that it's okay to go through phases and the sun as an inspiration that you will rise again no matter how many times you go down. Remember, what you don't want will empower you to go after what you do want. Everything is working together for your greater good. At every moment, you are doing the best you can with where you are. Trust the process that allows you to evolve into more of who you are destined to become.

January 22

I am excited about my possibilities.

When you ask, the Universe may sometimes respond, "Stop, not yet, or wait." Don't be concerned. The answer is only letting you know the timing is not ideal, and better is available to you. Remember, your desires are never denied; they are only deferred until you align with what you want. Delays reveal that more work is needed to get better prepared to receive what you requested. Instead of getting frustrated about the timing or feeling discouraged about the block, expand your mindset. Build a better connection between what you believe and what you deserve. Your efforts to improve will bring more than you can imagine. Don't get stuck on the stop; get excited about the possibilities.

January 23

I am getting ready for my win.

Slow down, or you will skip the steps sent to set you up for success. Take a moment to acknowledge the positive transformations that can come from giving yourself time to rest and reset. Use the time to learn to listen more attentively to what your soul wants. Use the time to develop the compassion needed to restore important relationships. Use the time to create more clarity about what you envision for your life. Use the time to imagine more significant dreams. Occasionally pausing, reorganizing, and praying for guidance, will keep you optimistic and patient while you progress. Sometimes the ability to rest and reset will make you ready for when you get your yes. Keep preparing for the momentum you are gaining. Relax; what you want is already done.

January 24

I am releasing my limits and welcoming my win.

Sometimes it isn't about your desires; it is about the beliefs blocking what you think you deserve. A scarcity mindset delays abundance. Reliving hurt keeps you from healing pain. The need for validation traps you in someone else's idea of your worth. When you remove what holds you back, what you need will show up. Shorten the timeframe of manifestation by preparing yourself mentally, physically, spiritually, or emotionally for what you want. Impatience makes you skip the steps to success. Your dreams will materialize faster when you release the limits or conditions you have around them. Remember, you are a powerful creator; it is your job to ask then get ready to welcome the win.

January 25

I am capable and COPE-able.

It is your responsibility to keep encouraging yourself to live the best you can by focusing on your happiness. Yes, it takes time to adjust to constantly changing circumstances, but don't forget to simultaneously create the improvements you want to see. Instead of worrying, remember your ability to produce solutions. Instead of getting frustrated, be mindful of the energy it takes from you. Instead of focusing on the past, embrace the possibilities of your future. Trust you have what it takes to create your breakthrough from any breakdowns. Believe in your blessings, yourself, and your miracles. Start each day with gratitude; it will enhance your outlook on life. Mindfully living can improve your capability and develop your COPE-ability.

January 26

I am deserving of success.

When you give in to negative emotions like shame, unworthiness, or guilt, you challenge your well-being. Healing begins when you choose to prioritize your good feelings. Yes, circumstances can make you temporarily lose sight of who you are, but they unfold to help you remember what you are capable of creating. You, like everyone else, deserve to achieve whatever you desire. There will always be something that will test you; never let it distract you from where you are going and the highest vision for your life. Your daily choices can empower you to reconnect with who you are and what you know about your success. Decide daily where to focus your energy. Everything you need to be happy is already within you. Concentrate on the emotions that encourage your thriving.

January 27

I am forgiving myself and focusing forward.

Forgive yourself for the times you stayed stuck in the past instead of focusing on the present. Forgive yourself for feeling like a victim instead of deciding to go for your victory. Forgive yourself for the journey you took to understand what you deserve. Forgive yourself for staying in situations that made you feel helpless but showed you that you were already enough. Forgive yourself for the pace it takes for you to live your purpose. Forgive yourself as many times as you need to develop the self-compassion it takes to keep going. Self-love begins with remembering you are always doing the best you can with what you know. Forgive yourself and free your soul to find what you need to flourish.

January 28

I am welcoming the best life has to offer.

Whenever you have a doubtful moment, reflect on the improvements you made and the mindset you transformed to get where you are. Give yourself credit for the abundance you created from what you had. Celebrate the mountains you conquered and the strength it built. Be gratified that the stormy seas you navigated through never deterred you. Today step back and honestly look at how amazing you are and all you have accomplished. Remember, your wins are your work. No one can take that accomplishment from you. Keep making an effort to become a better version of yourself, and don't give up on your happiness. You do enough. You are enough. You deserve the best life has to offer.

January 29

I am going for my happiness.

When your climb is challenged, you have to believe you can get to the top, even though your way feels blocked. Sometimes you must lose what you think you love, watch familiar things become strange, and feel comfort zones transform to the unfamiliar, all before you continue your climb. The hardest part of any struggle is learning to think and feel differently while trying to stay hopeful. Yes, the first step upward will be your most demanding, but it will also be your most rewarding. Don't let the thought of creating change defeat you before you even take action. Elevation requires separation from what does not serve your journey to more joy. You cannot grow big, playing small. Go for your happiness; you have what it takes to reach the top. Start climbing, my friend.

January 30

I am trusting the process.

Your confusion will be replaced with clarity. Your pursuit of peace will reveal the path to your purpose. Your worry will show what you are truly worth. Your lack will level you up to more. Your blocks will make way for abundant blessings. Your doubt will reveal what you should do. Your closed-door will redirect you to the right path. Nothing you go through is permanent; everything is part of a bigger plan. Believe that the positive change you want can happen in an instant. Remember, nothing is ever taken away without being replaced with better. More is always trying to make its way to you. Get ready to accept the bountiful blessings coming because you deserve them. Trust everything is always working out for you.

January 31

I am appreciating and celebrating every step I take forward.

Today is a great day to count your blessings from the past month. Take a moment to stop, look, and love what showed up. Stop and feel gratitude for what you overcame to get to where you are. Look and observe how beautifully your progress has unfolded. Love and accept who you are becoming. You adapted to the circumstances, and you created improvements the best way you knew how. Trust you are always doing the best you can. Celebrate your progress because transformation is never easy. Appreciate every step you make forward. You committed to your happiness, and you kept growing and going. You did that!

February 01

I am joyously working on who I need to be.

This month I am focused on who I AM.

I am loving, and I am loved.

I am appreciative, and I am appreciated.

I am a blessing, and I am blessed.

I am inspiring, and I am inspired.

I am respectful, and I am respected.

I am supportive, and I am supported.

I am abundant, and I am abundance.

I am creative, and I am a creator.

At this moment, I am the best I can be.

February 02

I am making great choices for my happiness.

Today release yourself from the burdens of your past. Let it all go by leaving the experiences behind you where they belong. You have what it takes to move beyond what others did or did not do. Find your freedom from needing explanations, apologies, closure, validation, or answers you may never get. Shift your focus to how you want to feel in the now. Recognize your joy is your responsibility. Discern when to fight and when to focus forward. Learn to control where your attention goes, and your desires will expand. Peace arrives when you realize your choices create your happiness. Always have faith in who you are and where you are going. You decide what you create for your future.

February 03

I am already whole.

Open your heart to the wholeness of who you are. Find your inner peace, and it will reveal your purpose. Allow your gratitude to guide you with creating your abundance. Use your strength to uncover your capabilities. Work on your limits and you will master the significant blessings coming your way. Let all that you have lived empower you to build the life you want. Trust your desires are arranged and are already on the way. They are waiting for you to be ready to collect in full. You are capable of doing what's needed to manifest it all. Work on who you are, and you will be guided and supported to where you want to go. Life never blocks your blessings; it only provides the experiences that prepare you to receive them. Your journey is worth it when you enjoy it.

February 04

I am learning and leveling up.

You weren't abandoned; you were being guided to find your self-love. You weren't rejected; you were being shown how to heal what you don't face. You weren't blocked; you were being redirected to better. You weren't delayed; you were being slowed down to discover what you deserve. You weren't held back; you were being pulled to a path of purpose. You weren't taken from; you were given an opportunity to create more. Trust that what you are going through is helping you refine your wants. Try not to question why this is happening to you; instead, focus on what is emerging for you. Every season has a reason for your triumph. Be determined to win with what you are given. You are destined for success.

February 05

I am manifesting miracles.

No matter how the day unfolds, look at it with positivity. Let today's mood be praising, thanking, rejoicing, and celebrating. Praising for all the spontaneous blessings showing up for you. Thanking for the abundance flowing smoothly to you. Rejoicing for what you have overcome to get to your place of peace. Celebration for everything working out for you. Your life is a blessing. Acknowledge the big, small, good, challenging, confusing, clarifying, and you will always keep growing and moving forward. Believe everything is as it should be for you to create better. Your mood can manifest your miracles. Good energy brings excellent possibilities. Trust today will be the best day ever!

February 06

I am blessed with what I need to move forward.

At this moment, you are blessed with everything you need to move forward. You delay the manifestation when you doubt it will materialize. Release the limiting thoughts and unlock the blessings. Remember, if it's not the right time, you can't force it. If it's yours, you cannot lose it. If it's meant to be, you can't miss it. When it's your time, you cannot stop it. You have asked; trust it will be given. More is already on the way to you. You are sent exactly what you need when you are ready to receive it. Trust you are being positioned for your desires. Instead of being impatient, focus on getting prepared. Remember, keep the faith; big things can happen in short timeframes.

February 07

I am grateful for my progress.

Remember to celebrate your growth. Everything you have, and where you are right now, was once a desire. Where you are is enough; what you have is enough; what you do is enough. Be grateful; you are always moving forward. Acknowledge your efforts. When you appreciate what you have, you will unlock what you need to create more. Never let what is yet to be, distract you from what has already manifested. Take a moment to embrace what you have accomplished and celebrate the work you have done to change and create your abundance. Praise how far you have courageously traveled to move away from where you were. You have a lot around you to fill you with gratitude. Slow down and appreciate your progress. You did that!

February 08

I am joyful on my journey.

Surrendering to the process is not about giving up on your dreams; it is letting go of how you think they should materialize. Release how you believe it must unfold and focus on the 'why' you want your desires to manifest. Things may not always go according to your plan, but trust that there is a Divine plan, one that is in service of your highest good. Sometimes what you think is blocking you is actually blessing you with bigger opportunities. Try a new approach, focus on being joyful on the journey to what you want, and your dreams will materialize faster. Embrace the twists and turns along the way; they are leading you to the most beautiful places. Stay patient with the process. Believe that no matter what happens, things are always working out for you.

February 09

I am releasing and making room to receive.

Release your grip on the little, and more will manifest. Release the need to control how it should go and tune in for the inspired action to get it done. Release the limiting beliefs about what you think you deserve and permit bigger blessings to be created. Release any hurt or disappointment, and welcome the healing trying to get through the walls you built. Allow yourself to heal from the past. Allow yourself to embrace the possibilities of the future. Allow yourself to feel whole in the now. Allow yourself to keep going by remaining hopeful and optimistic. Allow yourself to see the life you want is possible. Allow yourself to dream bigger. Sometimes you have to release before you can allow more.

February 10

I am trusting that what I pray for is a done deal.

When you focus on better, you will get better. Everything starts with you and how you feel about yourself and your potential. Believe you are divinely supported and release the worry. Expect good news, answered prayers, breakthroughs, opened doors, and miracles. Trust things will work out in your favor. The supportive connections you wish for are being arranged for you. The breakthrough you are looking for is aligning sooner than you can imagine. The prosperity you are patiently waiting for is being packaged and positioned. Remember, the miracle you are expecting can manifest at any instant. The minute you trust that what you are praying for is a done deal, it's the moment it gets delivered.

February 11

I am going for it all.

You should never have to demonstrate your worth to anyone; stop trying. Prove it to yourself by believing you have enough, and you give enough. Your value never diminishes because of your experiences; it is revealed because you learn to define your worth. Trust something good is always happening for you, even when you cannot see it. When you believe you are worthy of all, you will begin to receive all. You are valuable enough to deserve more. You are brave enough to demand more. You are strong enough to go after more. You are smart enough to find solutions to produce more. You are capable enough to create more. You are prepared enough to receive more. More than you think is possible for you. My friend, go for it all.

February 12

I am aligning with what I desire.

Your impatience may be doubt in what you believe you deserve. When you rush results, you miss out on the reason for the delay. Just because progress has slowed doesn't mean your blessings were stopped. When you are made to wait, understand that you are guided to prepare before your circumstances gain momentum. Work through your challenges by focusing on the answers. Use the wait to acknowledge your growth, improve your well-being, concentrate on what you can change, and let go of what you cannot. Don't waste the in-between time worrying; make it work in your favor by adding to your requests. Trust everything you want, and more will manifest right on time. Remember, you are a powerful creator of solutions.

February 13

I am a creator, not a carrier.

Every phase of your life is designed to teach you how to level up to more. Remember, you don't have to keep carrying the painful situations you have conquered from one chapter into the next. When you release the hurt from the past, you develop the skills to create what you want for your future. You are meant to expand your possibilities from your experiences. Before you level up, make time to reflect on the great job you are doing. Trust a better version of you will unfold for every chapter of your life. Remember, your past is a point of reference, not a place of residence. Release and keep moving forward. Appreciate your efforts, celebrate your progress, and embrace who you are becoming. You are a creator, not a carrier.

February 14

I am embracing my purpose.

Limitations, experiences, talents, purpose, and destiny are all part of a Divine plan. Your limitations are released through your experiences. Your experiences reveal your talents. Expressing your talents support your purpose. Pursuing your purpose will guide you closer to the path of your destiny. Every up, down, yes, and no teaches you how to master unlocking your full potential. Your thriving is connected to your unique expression of your abilities. Lifelong fulfillment begins with looking at the one thing unique to you then use it to build the life you want. Most people overlook their talent because it is the most natural thing for them to express or create. Acknowledging every aspect of you will unlock the best of you. Find what feeds your soul, and you will flourish.

February 15

I am focused forward.

It is okay to get nostalgic from time to time. When you look back, don't try to focus on what went wrong; instead, concentrate on what you have accomplished or improved. Give yourself credit for the work you have done to change old patterns, overcome adversity, and transformed how and what you created. Remember, you deserve all you believe is possible. You are very capable of having everything you can imagine for yourself. Happy people enjoy where they are. Smart people build upon what they have experienced to craft the future they want. Fulfilled people know that everything is working together for their highest good. Choose to work every day at being happy, smart, and fulfilled. Trust you are always moving forward.

February 16

I am capable and creative enough to succeed.

Overthinking can originate from self-doubt, past outcomes, and challenging experiences. When your thought process is focused on what can go wrong, it blocks your ability to find solutions. Survival mode prevents you from seeing you are already thriving. You are capable and creative enough to succeed, and you already have what you need to find a way forward. The actions you are taking, the inner work you are doing, all will pay off soon. Keep believing in yourself and your prayers. You have what it takes; just keep going. Release the doubt and keep trusting the process. Time loses its power when your focus is happiness, not results. Trust in Divine timing.

February 17

I am a powerful creator.

Unlock your full potential by concentrating on your possibilities rather than your pain. Everyone has a past where someone has wronged them, or something did not go according to plan. Staying there locks you into victim mode and keeps you away from happiness. Switch to victor mode by accepting you are more than your past and worthy of a great future. You cannot expect blessings for things you aren't committed to creating. Change starts in the now. Stay dedicated to your happiness, and you will build a bigger and better life vision. Stay committed to self-compassion, and you will invite more support. Stay steadfast at creating abundance, and you will be prosperous. Stay showing up for your success and trust what you desire is yours. You are a powerful creator.

February 18

I am finding solutions all around me.

When a challenge occurs, don't get discouraged; stay focused. Delays only mean you are in the process of clarifying and fine-tuning your desires. Life is about sifting through and sorting out who you are and what you want. Trials help you define what happiness and fulfillment really mean to you. You must first have a problem to solve before you have the enjoyment of the solution. Don't panic; pray. Don't worry; worship. Don't cry; create. Don't give up; keep going. Don't have a break down; take a breath. Don't quit; pause and reset. Don't blow up; bless the situation. At this moment, you have a chance to make a choice that creates change. The unfolding is where your miracles will happen.

February 19

I am fine-tuning my happiness and pursuing my prosperity.

Many people devote their lives to changing what's going on around them, and they fail to see the power to create what they want comes from within them. The abundance you want starts with finding your worth. The love you desire begins with understanding what you deserve. The peace you pursue originates from being present. Commit to developing the mindset you need to succeed. Work on creating your best self from the inside out. Trust you have all that you need to build abundance. Flow with life as you pursue your happiness. Remember, you are Divinely guided, supported, protected, and loved at all times. Take the time to adjust your inner dial to the frequency of what you seek.

February 20

I am expecting the best always.

Are you excitedly preparing for love, success, support, peace, or abundance to manifest? Remember, you are what you expect. The most powerful words to help with belief begin with "I am." Let your affirmation statements today be about what you desire in your life tomorrow. Say it, believe it, then welcome the guidance to create it. Expect the best, always. Use the next few words as often as needed to keep you motivated. "I am thankful for what is yet to come. I am expecting cleared paths, opened doors, and unlimited possibilities to keep thriving. I am celebrating the abundant opportunities of success that are showing up for me. I am delighting in the good flowing to me. I am rejoicing and declaring I have everything I need. Everything is always working out for me."

February 21

I am leaving the past where it belongs, behind me.

You cannot let desired experiences come to you if you don't move past what challenged you. Yes, you have been wounded, but it won't fully heal if you keep picking at the scar. It is natural to want to protect your heart, but you must find a way to let the past go and allow the good to unfold. Be mindful, the barriers you built to protect yourself can also block what you want to manifest. Make a change, be hopeful that everything is working out for you. Release the thoughts that do not serve your happiness and limit your possibilities. Welcome the pouring of prosperity and well-being into your life. Give your heart and soul the peace it seeks by trusting life is always on your side.

February 22

I am celebrating my wins.

Cycles of resilience, rejection, receiving, and redemption are all important to any successful journey. Resilience is where you learn your strength to bend without breaking. Rejection is where you are taught to reclaim your true worth. Receiving is where you use gratitude to focus on your blessings. Redemption is where you celebrate your triumphs. Learning to embrace change will help you easily transition through your life seasons. Trust that every up, down, back, and forth has a purpose of getting you clear about what your happiness truly means to you. Remember, when you are made to step back, life is setting you up to make leaps forward. Whatever stage you are in, know you have what it takes to get through them all. Keep going.

February 23

I am counting my blessings and praising my progress.

Take a second to consider what you see for yourself. Try not to allow your experiences to limit your perspective of what is possible. Some people are afraid, not because they fear the mountain, but because they do not trust they have what it takes to make it to the top. Remember, everyone is given what they need to succeed. Believe that your life can be better than you can currently imagine. Yes, you have stumbled, but you were supported and never fell off as you climbed. Take a moment today to count your blessings and celebrate your progress. If what you see now keeps you doubtful, don't believe it; it is your time to rise. Right now, you have enough to create more. Believe the top exists, and start ascending, my friend.

February 24

I am thankful for my blessings.

Don't let past experiences keep you stuck doubting your abilities. Consider every morning you wake up a new opportunity to start over, stronger and wiser than before. You must have the courage to pay attention to how you want to feel now and fuel what you can create tomorrow. Redirect your focus from what you are going through and start 'thanking' for your blessings. Every closed door is redirecting you to rewarding opportunities. Leave yesterday where it is. Appreciate today and begin it with optimistic thoughts, new habits, and better beliefs. Reclaim your happiness with thankfulness for the ability to live with purpose every day. How blessed are you to be given another chance to create what you want?

February 25

I am trusting things are working in my favor.

Doubt can keep you distracted from doing. Combat the feeling by choosing to have faith over fear. Fear keeps you stuck, and faith keeps you focused forward. Instead, concentrate on what is working in your favor. Use your gratitude to change any moment into one filled with grace. If you believe in the blessings coming, you won't stress about what is happening. With grace and gratitude, allow life to remove what does not serve your happiness. Clearing and creation require time. Remember, you never lose, you only learn who you are. How you choose to live your life makes you a winner. Trust things are working out for you.

February 26

I am leveling up to my promise.

You created a positive change from your challenges. You built bridges to your abundance by using the lessons you learned from lack. You opened doors to more after being blocked by the ones that closed on you. You overcame the setbacks sent to stop you from stepping forward and leveling up. You manifested miracles from meager beginnings. Always believe that life is for you and working with you to bring your desires. When you think things are falling apart, understand they are only falling into place. Sometimes foundations need to break for you to rebuild better. Life will upgrade and transform you for your promise. You are an amazing person creating a miraculous life. Never forget to celebrate your efforts.

February 27

I am in control of what I create.

To live your best life, you must be your best self. Being your best self is not about resisting but embracing your power to create change. Remember, in every situation; you have control over whether you react or respond. Survival is when you react to your circumstances without much consideration for your actions. Reacting gives the situation control over you. Thriving is when you respond to your situation with carefully thought-out actions. This response provides you with control of the life you build. Yes, life happens, but how you respond to the setback creates the setup. You will always meet obstacles; only you can control what is yielded after. You can retreat and stay small or push forward and build big. Always go big. You are Divinely supported on your journey.

February 28

I am forgiving and moving forward.

When you haven't forgiven someone, you believe they owe you something. This creates a need for resolution that leaves you stuck in the past. What if the explanation, clarity, or apology never came? Then it is up to you to release yourself from being trapped in the emotional cycle. Forgive, move forward, and stop wishing it was different. Yes, you were hurt, but it is your responsibility to heal and pursue peace. Releasing, healing and forgiveness are necessary to step forward to where you want to go. Don't let what is behind you prevent you from planting solid roots, planning for your future, and trusting in your happiness. No one owes you anything. You, however, owe yourself everything, especially a life full of joy.

February 29

I am loving myself more and more.

You are constantly making choices that write the story of your life. Take it one decision at a time, one day at a time. Give yourself room to make mistakes because it is how you learn. Encourage yourself by celebrating your progress. Keep supporting your dreams by doing despite the occasional doubt. Acknowledge your wins and keep going. Only you can stay committed to your happiness. Allow yourself to love yourself a little bit more every day. Make your change from the most empowered emotional state you can be in – gratitude. Believe in who you are and what you deserve and never ever wait to be happy. Trust at this moment; you are completely worthy of everything you desire. Put faith in your power of creation.

March 01

I am welcoming my well-being.

This March, I am centering myself with gratitude for my blessings. As I release the thoughts that do not serve my happiness, I welcome the pouring of prosperity and well-being into my life. My heart and soul are at peace because I trust that I am Divinely supported at all times. I am faith-FULL that all my needs are met. I am focused on my natural ability to create. I know that I am a powerful point of attraction, and everything that I desire is ALL ready to manifest for me. I am always expanding, growing, and moving closer to my desires. I know that I am already loved. I am already blessed. I am already abundant. I am already happy. I am already supported. I am already receiving more. Everything is ALL ways working out for me.

March 02

I am connecting to who I am.

Self-love is the feeling, and self-care is the action. You can have self-love but fall short in your self-care practice. Going within is a form of self-love. Don't neglect your moments of stillness. It connects you to who you are and helps improve what needs attention. You cannot course correct if you don't know how to direct the driver. Get still and connect with who is steering your life. You must put yourself first so that you can then be the best for others. "Self-first" is not selfish when you take the time to create habits that support how you feel and the thriving you want in your life. When you align your positive intentions with inspired actions, your happiness will blossom beyond your imagination. Change is fully appreciated when it comes from within.

March 03

I am using what I am given to create my desires.

You can't worry about lack and expect to receive abundant blessings. You can't doubt your ability to build the life you want and believe you are a creator. You can't stay stuck in the past and desire a different future. You can't close off your heart and be open to love. You cannot create a new life with old mindsets. Change your life with three principles: vision, intention, and action. Vision - because you must first believe in where you are going before you go. Intention - because you must be clear about why you want your happiness to grow. Action - because it is important to work on yourself while you make requests. Develop all these as habits, and you will create the life you desire.

March 04

I am being protected and provided for.

Find your best self by focusing on the blessings showing up in your life. If you're feeling impatient, ground yourself with gratitude. Gratitude for how far you have traveled emotionally, spiritually, and mentally. Gratitude for the strength it took to overcome and triumph to get to this moment. Gratitude that you are miraculously being protected and provided for in all areas of your life. Gratitude that you have what it takes to keep going. When you ground yourself with gratitude, greatness will manifest daily. Stay committed to creating your joy and abundance. When you operate from your happy self, life becomes more manageable. Remember, you are already blessed. Trust your desires are on the way.

March 05

I am using my faith to keep climbing to the top.

Having faith does not mean you will have it easy; it is about finding comfort in knowing you will eventually succeed despite setbacks. Remember, no one is exempt from trying times. Keep putting up a good fight to stay in the race, and don't quit because you feel challenged. Say goodbye to what needs to go and release it with grace. Say hello to the blessings on the way and welcome them with gratitude. Always believe in your possibilities. Use the power of faith to keep climbing even when you cannot see the top. Trust what you diligently work for will materialize soon. At this moment, life is working for you, with you, and ahead of you. Have faith obstacles are being cleared, and doors are opening. Keep going; Source has your back.

March 06

I am focused on being better.

The Universe conspires in your favor when you commit to your happiness. Dreams always start as a seed or idea. Yes, miracles manifest from dirt, but the seed must be lovingly nurtured and encouraged to thrive. The infinite possibilities of what you can create are based on your actions, your relationship with yourself, and the attention you place on your emotional wealth. Use what you are given to grow your prosperity. Remember seeds take time to mature. Getting impatient will not make them flourish any faster. Keep trusting that your planting is consistently producing, even when you do not see results. Give your seed time to push through the dirt and transform into a harvest that thrives through any season. What is for you always shows up at the right time.

March 07

I am creating the life I want.

Happiness requires life-long training; don't get stuck trying to figure it all out at once. It is impossible to take all of your classes in one sitting or from one teacher. Focus on passing the test in front of you; it is preparing you for the next step. Work on one phase, master it, then move on to another. Lessons are never about where you are; it is about discovering and embracing who you need to be to get to where you are going. Appreciate the wisdom gained from all your experiences. Without them, you would not have been able to move forward. Like a video game, every victory unlocks what lessons must be learned to level up. Focus on what you need to master at this moment to get to your next chapter. You are always writing the story of your life, make it a great one full of wins.

March 08

I am grounded in gratitude.

Daily, your experiences can take, push, or pull from you mentally and emotionally, which can be draining to your energy. A great way to keep yourself re-energized and balanced is to set a positive intention for your day consistently. Being positive does not mean that things will always be okay; it just means you will purposefully be okay no matter the circumstances. Let your intention be one focused on creating good emotions throughout the day. Emotions like gratitude help you stay grounded and dedicated to your success. When you put your well-being first, you can then serve others from the overflow. You have to be good before you can be of any good to anyone. Self-first is not selfish; it is how you set yourself up to thrive in any circumstance.

March 09

I am releasing my focus on the pace.

Reality can sometimes be challenging. However, it is important to make peace with where you are while working on where you want to go. It's not about settling for your life; it's about finding solutions through a positive and hopeful attitude. Big possibilities cannot be created from limited thinking. Today, set aside the distraction of your difficulties and focus on your progress, not the pace you are winning the race. You walked miles without realizing the significance of the steps you were taking. Marvel at how much you have grown. Be amazed by the miracle of how you are transforming your life. It's in the moments you choose to celebrate; you learn to experience the joy of your journey.

March 10

I am deserving of the love I give.

You cannot expect someone to fully love you when you are partially committed to your well-being. It is your responsibility to be clear about how you share and receive love. The best way to improve your beliefs about love is through a consistent practice of self-care and self-compassion. Never let a poorly executed chapter taint your entire love story. Real love starts with understanding how to love yourself more. Remember, you are lovable and amazing. Don't allow someone's actions to take that belief from your heart. Everyone has it challenging from time to time, but that doesn't mean your happiness becomes less important. Every heart deserves to be loved, and every face deserves a smile. Keep smiling and loving, my friend. You deserve the love you give.

March 11

I am making the most of my journey.

No one is ever ready for the tests they face, yet they figure out how to forge forward. No one is ever prepared to carry burdens, but they must trust it cultivates their strength to survive. No one's life is ever perfect, but they learn to develop grace through their mistakes. Hope is one of the most powerful feelings you can have; it will help you navigate it all. Make the most of your journey by developing your discernment, practicing patience, and acknowledging you are constantly being blessed and guided along the way. It is up to you to find joy on the journey you are taking. Life is about doing your best on the ride, not the arrival. Start with celebrating your progress.

March 12

I am patient and faithful.

What you are praying for wants to align with you. Stop pushing it away with doubt and impatience. You cannot create with faith and wait in fear. Today reconnect with your trust by believing in Divine timing. Instead of worrying about when it will happen, try thanking for its delivery. Every experience is designed to prepare you to collect. Hearts must be opened to receive, shoulders strengthened to carry, and mindsets mastered to build abundance. Trust your request is being worked on, and you are moving closer to your more every day. Your thriving is already created, do the work to get yourself ready. Today make room for your delivery. Remember, big, beautiful blessings can manifest in short timeframes. Stay patient and faithful.

March 13

I am stepping into my highest potential.

When it feels like things are falling apart, don't worry, trust it is all coming together for your highest good. When you prayed for more, the answer was your inner growth. You are being shown how to build a better foundation, which means letting go of what's not supporting you. Remember, right now you are exactly where you need to be. Stay hopeful. Focus your attention on the things working out, not on why things aren't happening. Life is only trying to reveal that where you are is not the furthest you can reach, and you are destined for more. Allow yourself to reach for better. Don't let comfort on the lower ground prevent you from stepping into your highest potential. Rise, my friend, rise.

March 14

I am choosing to have faith.

Today refuse to let the doubt within you win. Fight the feeling by believing in your capabilities. Clear the doubt that is in the way of what you deserve. Trust you have what it takes to pursue your possibilities. You are doing the best you can with what you know. Use the affirmation: "I am choosing to have faith." Repeat it as many times as you need and conquer the doubt by doing what makes you feel your best. Believe you are worthy. Believe you have the power to overcome. Believe your dreams are possible. Believe you are enough, and you do enough. Believe you can write a new life story. Believe things are working out for you. Believe everything you asked for is aligning for you. Most of all, believe you can create the life you want.

March 15

I am doing the best I can.

In the moments you feel discouraged, take a deep breath, and ask yourself what is needed to regain momentum. Do you physically need to rest and reenergize? Do you mentally need to realign with your positive thoughts and emotions? Do you spiritually need to feel inspired by rebuilding your faith in your future? Do you need to emotionally find what feels good? Every situation has a different need and requires a different response. Be patient as you discover what will encourage you to keep moving forward. Don't judge yourself for needing a break. Figuring out what enables you to thrive will help you triumph. Always be kind to yourself and remember you are doing the best you can. Self-compassion will always help you find what you need to succeed.

March 16

I am Divinely supported.

From the instant you create a desire to the moment it materializes, there is a momentum that needs to build. Everything you seek requires time to greet you where you are trying to meet it. It is your job to step up and align with your needs to bring them closer to you. Paths are not cleared until you walk through them. Doors aren't opened until you knock, and obstacles aren't removed until you release your limits. Don't worry about what you think might happen; focus on what is happening and do your best to create solutions. You have always been provided for one way or another. Believe you will get the Divine support you need and keep going. Remember, miracles always manifest fully. Trust the process.

March 17

I am not giving up on my happiness.

Many get distracted with the need for immediate resolution and spend little time meditating. You must occasionally go within to receive a Divinely guided answer. Move past reacting with only emotion and add mindfulness. Decisions based on fear can create chaos. Decisions made with discernment create what you want. You control how you respond. You have the power to stop reacting to the life you are living and start creating the life you desire. Peace will only be found when your heart and head align for the solutions you seek. Today take the time to listen and align with your well-being before you respond. Be intentional with your choices.

March 18

I am trusting the process.

Gratitude will make every day a great day. It expands your awareness and helps you experience every moment with freedom, creativity, and joy. The more grateful you are for what you have, the more you can create. You are always attracting the support and resources needed to complete your vision. Trust the Universe is working behind the scenes to move you in the direction of your dreams. When you ground your soul with gratefulness, you become a magnet for all good things. Use the delays to master your commitment and determination to succeed. Don't give up; keep going. You have what it takes. You're not far from what you desire. It will happen soon. Get ready to receive more than you can imagine.

March 19

I am trusting in my abilities, and I am leveling up.

Self-confidence is developed with each decision made. When your choices have the desired outcome, you generate trust in your abilities; that's winning. When your choices have unwanted results, you learn what you are capable of creating; that's wisdom. Both help you grow and master life. Every decision cultivates your discernment and helps you level up to more. Keep developing your relationship with yourself and your choices; it will improve your beliefs about what you can achieve. Manifestation happens the moment you align yourself with what you want. Get familiar with who you are, and the decisions you make will get easier.

March 20

I am strong.

You are doing a great job with your efforts to change old habits and release situations that do not serve your evolution. When you feel like giving up, remember why you began to take this path. Applaud yourself for your dedication. Don't quit right before the breakthrough. Start with prioritizing how you want to feel and use it to create what is important to you. When you make happiness your primary focus, nothing will prevent you from crossing the finish line. Remember your progress by focusing on what's yet to come. There is always more, and you deserve more; trust you are already creating more. Keep showing up, stay positive, and keep moving forward without looking back. You are blessed and Divinely supported on your journey.

March 21

I am deserving of all.

Forgive yourself for the times you stayed stuck in the past. Credit yourself for the courage it took to move forward. Believe you can create your future. Forgive yourself for feeling like you lost. Credit yourself for getting back in the race to pursue your victory. Develop the self-compassion that is needed to forgive as many times as necessary. Whatever you are experiencing right now, have faith that it is part of a plan designed to bring you what you desire. Remember, failure is part of learning how to forge forward, and your blocks are part of developing your beliefs. All circumstances, trials, and triumphs become necessary to one journey - your journey. Never be afraid to start from where you are and go for all. Trust you are supported and protected.

March 22

I am hopeful for big blessings.

The Universe is answering. It may not be what you want, but it is always what you need. Wants are what you think will make you happy. Needs are necessary for your soul to move towards thriving. When you ask for blessings, focus on your needs, it will lead to the manifestation of your wants. You are constantly expanding and moving closer to all your desires. Don't lose faith right before the fruition; focus on what needs to get done for the miracle to manifest. Sometimes one request is only the beginning of a larger vision that needs time to unfold. Use the time to understand the magnitude of your worth. Remember, growth is happening, even if it appears as slow as one percent at a time. Get hopeful for the biggest blessing you can imagine.

March 23

I am celebrating my blessings.

At this instant, you have so much to be thankful for. You are surrounded by people who love you despite how you feel about where you are. You are triumphing over battles no one knew you were fighting. You are healing from the hurt that held you back from going after your ALL. You are shedding the old and creating new blessings. You are manifesting more in every moment. If you don't currently see your miracle, be patient. Remember, when you are down to nothing, the Universe is always up to something. Trust the magic will manifest. Remember, you are always supported. Have faith change is happening, even if you do not see it. Celebrate all that you are doing to create the life you desire.

March 24

I am focused on the good within me.

Facing past trauma can be scary; however, it is necessary to be happy and move forward. Work on you; it will get you to your destination. Yes, healing can take longer than what caused the pain, but choices made from the filters of unresolved hurt can keep you stuck. Focus on your positive attributes and your unlimited potential. They will help you push past your pain to create beauty from a place of love. You owe it to yourself to heal. Do the work to get ready for where you are going; it will be worth it. You must put effort into your healing by remembering your wholeness. Prepare to live the happiness you are creating. Everything you've been through is preparing you for a breakthrough.

March 25

I am giving myself credit for my progress.

Today, go within and focus on what you need. Take a minute to re-prioritize, recharge, and reset before you get tired and want to quit. You may need to pause and figure out the lesson you are missing before you level up. You may need to renew and strengthen your commitment to why you want the win. Each experience will require a different you before you make more progress. Remember, you are constantly moving forward and doing the best you can with what you know at every moment. Trust everything is unfolding perfectly, and there is power in finding the purpose for your current position. Acknowledge how far you have traveled and keep going.

March 26

I am focused on my fruitful future.

Sometimes happiness is a choice between fight or flight. Only you can decide if you believe in the possibility of your dreams or worry about your ability to have what you want. Faith is your fight. Fear is your flight. Before you give up, appreciate that you are given another chance to create the life you desire every morning. Don't let doubt deter you from actively creating your vision. Find your confidence by believing that challenges are always conquered and miracles always manifest. You were not Divinely guided this far, to be forgotten. No matter what you face, you have to believe in a better future before you move forward. Stay faith FULL, my friend. Only you can fight for your future.

March 27

I am in control of what I can create.

You can control whether you react or respond. Reacting to your circumstances without consideration for your actions gives the situation control over you. Responding to your situation with carefully thought-out actions puts you in control of what you create. You have the power to choose how you win and make things work out for you. Happiness happens when you activate your power of choice. You can choose to empower yourself and move forward with faith. Focusing on love can lighten the burden of hurt. Focusing on gratitude can provide peace in a moment of uncertainty. Don't give up; you have what it takes to be happy despite what you see. Stop reacting. Start responding.

March 28

I am living in the moment.

Miracles always manifest when you aren't paying attention. When you release the focus on when and how your blessings will arrive, only then will they show up and surprise you. Move past questioning why things aren't better and allow what is unfolding to usher in your desires. Giving up control requires spiritual, mental, and emotional effort. Your work is in who you become while you wait. Make room in your life to receive what you want. Don't let your doubt get in the way. Remember, you are a magnet for love, peace, abundance, success, and joy. Trust things are always working out for you. Master your focus on what you are doing now and how it contributes to where you are going. Being present is the best present you can give your future self.

March 29

I am destined to reach the top.

You must know pain to know love. Know struggle to recognize success. Be at the bottom to understand the importance of the rise to the top. Be thankful for it all and keep growing and going. Use hope and faith to strengthen you for the journey. Hope that nothing remains the same. Faith that you are intended for the best. Never doubt your destiny or ability to manifest the life you want. Believe you are worthy of every bit of the success you are creating. Stay focused, keep improving, and climbing. You are doing a great job. You deserve to have it all. Trust you are doing the best you can at all times. Today look at what you have accomplished and celebrate that. Climb, my friend, climb. Every step will be worth it.

March 30

I am always moving forward.

Progress can be subtle, and it requires patience. It is so quiet you don't notice when you made it to where you wanted to go. The commitment to the journey can be challenging. Keep going, trusting, and asking for the mental clarity to overcome what holds you back. Before you know it, the dark days will be behind you, and the dreams you worked on will be happening for you. Yes, growth can be exhausting, but rest as much as you need along the way. Trust you are always moving forward, and where you are standing today will be behind you tomorrow. Don't let the challenges keep you from going after your all. Remember, the Universe is continually working to remove the obstacles you cannot see.

March 31

I am prepared to receive my blessings.

Say thank you to every door you knocked on that didn't open. Rejoice that it stopped you from getting into places where you did not belong. Remember, you aren't needed to open the doors already opened for you. You don't have to clear the paths already cleared for you. You aren't needed to build the bridges already built for you. Stop doing the work that isn't meant for you to do. Your job is to focus on the mindset that prepares you to receive the blessings of where you are going. What is meant for you will open and welcome you when you get there. Believe in your dreams and release the need to know how they will manifest. Trust things are falling into place.

April 01

I am already whole.

This April, I am committed to my happiness. I am pursuing my peace. I am letting in love. I am aligning with abundance. I am grounded in gratitude. I am releasing the old and embracing the new. I am making great choices and improving my life. I am developing the mindset that levels me up to more. I am celebrating my progress. I am welcoming miracles manifesting. I am praying with gratitude for the fruitful future that is already prepared for me. I invite healing, cleared paths, opened doors, and limitless harvest. I embrace the goodness in my life and diligently work to create more. I am thankful for the daily provisions and manifested abundance that is making its way to me.

April 02

I am a beautiful, blessed being, and I deserve good things.

Yes, you had to be in survival mode yesterday, but you can choose to thrive today. Don't let the past make you question your value. Anything that is taken away is always replaced with substantially better. Focus on what's showing up in the present to reveal your true worth. You are a beautiful blessed human being deserving of all good things. To get good things, you have to allow yourself to receive them. Open up and permit yourself to become the person that receives abundant blessings. Start with believing you are worthy before you receive it. Remember to support your thriving by speaking kindly and compassionately to yourself. Make your words life-giving.

April 03

I am moving closer to my dreams.

The Universe knows what you want. It knows right where you are, and it knows exactly where you need to be. Even though things aren't entirely how you want them to go, trust your circumstances have a purpose. Focus on the lesson to be learned, the skill to be developed, or the person you need to become before moving forward. Use your experiences to fuel your desire to create more, not determine your future potential. Sometimes growth requires ending something, leaving it behind, and lightening up before you level up. If you truly understand that what's yours will come when you are ready, you will release your focus on the clock and work on your worthiness. Trust the process.

April 04

I am blessed, and more is manifesting for me.

You cannot fully manifest your dreams with doubt in your heart. Improve what you believe you can achieve by releasing the old narratives that make you think you aren't worthy of your desires. Challenging experiences did not make you incapable; they gave you clarity about your ability to pursue your possibilities. Remember, if you can dream it, you can create it. Don't let anyone tell you differently. When you believe that better is possible, more will manifest. Everything you need is already provided for you, and more will be there as you progress. Keep your expectations positive by professing powerful words of prosperity and potential into your life.

April 05

I am on the right path to my happiness.

Decide today to be response-able for your future. You may not be responsible for hurt in your past or control the circumstances in the present, but you can choose to make your well-being a priority. Only you can select the path to your happiness. Today let your thoughts focus on alignment with what makes your soul flourish. You are the only one that can recognize the wholeness of your heart. You are the only one that can master the mindset that creates the happiness you want. You are the only one that can plant the seeds that blossom into abundance. You are the only one that can pursue the life you desire. Everything you need is already within you. Align and thrive.

April 06

I am making responsible choices.

It is human nature to focus on your actions and discard the importance of your decisions. Life isn't only about taking action to improve a situation; it is also about the quality of choices you make. Moving forward requires releasing the habits that limit your mental and emotional well-being. Some experiences are designed to break old patterns and unleash your wholeness. Never allow mistakes to take your confidence or hold you back from moving forward. Keep focusing on the quality of one choice at a time. You have the power to stop reacting to the life you are living and start creating the life you desire. Remember, you never lose; you are always learning.

April 07

I am healing and thriving.

Consider your heart the seed of your life because what you hold in it will be what grows. What you reap is based on your actions, relationship with self, and the attention you place on your emotional health. You cannot harvest abundance with a mindset of lack. You cannot create love with a heart heavy with resentment. You cannot produce peace sourced from chaos. Always plant in faith, not in fear. Yes, miracles manifest from nowhere, but your healing will help with thriving. Just as nature gives a seed everything it needs to grow; the Universe has given you everything you need to thrive. Trust in your abilities. You have what it takes to push through the dirt and blossom. Keep your seed flourishing by focusing on your emotional, spiritual, and mental well-being.

April 08

I am focused on creating solutions.

You can stop suffering when you start surrendering to the experiences sent to set you free from what burdens you. When you choose to hold onto the old by resisting the new, you make the transformation more tiring. Yes, the change might be challenging, but getting through it does not have to be complicated. Trust it is all unfolding for your highest good. Today instead of allowing the challenge to take your strength, focus on creating solutions. Don't let the fear of what could happen; make it that nothing happens. Push past your inner doubt by focusing on what you have already built for yourself. Everyone goes through changes, but what you create from it becomes your most significant victory.

April 09

I am already winning.

Keep praying for the skills to overcome and the ability to find your way through. Keep praying for the understanding to move beyond what holds you back from producing your prosperity. Keep praying to release the past and welcome the clarity to create your future. Keep praying for the healing and self-compassion that opens you up to love. Yes, there will be lessons to learn or self-work to be done; but believe in every moment your prayers will be answered, and you will be provided with what you need to triumph. Decide that no matter what comes your way, you already have the support and the skills needed to create your win. Trust things are always working out for your good. Remember, the Universe has your back and is silently moving your blessings into place.

April 10

I am unlimited potential.

The Universe is always trying to give you the experiences that guide you to the highest vision for your life. For every test or struggle, there is a better version of you being guided to emerge. You asked for more; trust that you are being directed to more. Your experiences are designed to reveal the true significance of your worth. Don't be so focused on what you think you want and miss the real blessing of who you are becoming. Concentrating on what you don't have will keep you from going after what you could have. Release the focus on your flaws and explore your possibilities. Understand your power to produce has unlimited potential. Today look at what you have accomplished and acknowledge you are capable of creating all that you desire.

April 11

I am exactly where I need to be.

Trust that you are exactly where you need to be right now. Your prayers can't be answered if you keep replacing your faith with fear. In accepting where you are, you acknowledge your progress and your work on your happiness. Always celebrate your commitment and effort to keep building the life you want. Only you can decide if this moment is filled with doubt about what you desire or gratitude about what you have achieved. Appreciation in every moment builds momentum for more miracles. To create the life you want, you must become dedicated to living the life you deserve. Stay hope FULL, faith FULL, and keep developing your fruit FULL future.

April 12

I am Divinely guided and supported.

When you ask for more, life will push, pull, and carry you there. Create your thriving by pushing yourself through your healing. Find your purpose by pulling yourself through the storms that develop your resilience. Reach your victory by acknowledging the Divine assistance carrying you across the finish line. Remember, you are always supported, protected, guided, and loved. Supported with resources to create the life you want. Protected from anything that gets in the way of your success. Guided to better after a breakdown. Loved when you felt abandoned with nowhere to go. Today, take a moment to recognize that something greater than you is silently sustaining your well-being.

April 13

I am committed to my happiness.

What you want will materialize. Be thankful that it is already unfolding in your life. Acknowledge its presence by crediting yourself as the creator. You are capable of producing everything you desire; stop doubting your efforts. Remember, happiness is not obtained when everything falls into place; it is experienced when you appreciate your efforts to make your miracles manifest. Be at peace with your pace and trust things are already working in your favor. Enjoy the process of creation, and you will be blessed with more results. Blessings are never late; they are always on time. Trust what you are working on is already a done deal. You are creator, keep creating.

April 14

I am aligning and flying.

Let go of how you think your life should be and pay attention to where it is showing you to go. You are destined to be more and have more. Working on anything worthwhile requires commitment and courage. Start with creating dreams that are significant enough to push you toward your fullest potential. Yes, believing in your possibilities can feel overwhelming, but don't let doubt creep in and convince you that you are on the brink of falling or failing. Now is not the time to play small. Go big by trusting that every step you take is supported. Take comfort in knowing your path will be cleared. Remember, what is meant for you will get to you. Step out in faith and trust you are not about to fall; you are about to fly. Let go, align, and fly.

April 15

I am resting, reenergizing, and remembering my why.

When your dreams begin to feel too far away to finish, don't immediately discard them. There is a difference between knowing when to rest and when to quit. Everyone occasionally feels like they don't want to keep fighting to make things happen. You are not alone. It is okay to get tired of working and waiting. If you find yourself in the middle of your manifestation, don't quit. Slow down and reenergize before you go. You have made significant improvements; focus on your progress. You may be one deliberate action away from completion. Where you are today is further than yesterday. Remember your why and continue your pursuit of happiness.

April 16

I am strong enough to improve my life.

You are doing the best you know with what you have learned. Forgive the version of yourself that did not know how to practice self-love and self-care consistently. You were only creating what you thought was right, not what was possible. Give yourself credit for choosing to do the work to produce the new results you currently see. Today, continue your journey. Give yourself more patience, love, and compassion. Patience to stick to the path that leads to prosperity. Self-love to know that you deserve what's right, not what's left. Self-compassion to keep releasing what does not serve your betterment. Trust you will create the change you desire. Transformation is a process that requires your persistence.

April 17

I am committed to my happiness.

What is meant for you will unfold in ways you could never expect or imagine. Nothing gets in the way of what is destined for you. Stop doubting what you deserve; start believing in what is becoming. Remember, life is not about perfection; it's about persistence when pursuing your path to what you desire. Be okay with your journey continuously changing. Your job is to transform with it. There will be 'go' days, 'do' days, 'stop' days, 'wait' days, 'rest' days, and 'reset' days. Whatever day is happening today, just do the best you can. That's the only thing that matters. It's your commitment to your happiness that will keep you moving forward. Keep showing up for your success. You've got this.

April 18

I am freely creating my future.

It is easy to keep replaying mistakes from your past. Your power of creation lies in this present moment. Don't let what's behind you prevent you from making your efforts count today. You are the one doing all the work to make your dreams come true; you cannot second guess yourself. Remember, you are strong, loving, intelligent, considerate, and you are not giving up on your happiness. Celebrate the actions you are taking. Find what feels good and use it to fuel and create the future you want. Greatness is ready to manifest in your life. It is time to remember who you are and what you are capable of doing. Allow your soul to lead the way. What you want tomorrow is created from what you do today. You are a powerful creator.

April 19

I am through the storm and thriving.

Remember, nothing in the past can hold you back when you stay committed to your happiness in the present. Change what you create by acknowledging your continued commitment to your well-being. Be proud of your persistence; you decided to get up today and fight for your right to be happy. Keep pushing through everything you are going through, and you will triumph. Trust you are doing all you can to create the future you want. Take it one decision at a time, one day at a time. Before you know it, you will be through the storm and thriving. Stay patient. Divine timing is perfect, and the plan is flawless. Trust things are already aligning for you.

April 20

I am saying yes to my blessings.

Today say yes to the progress and possibilities that are becoming a natural way of life for you. Say yes to the support that is available and abundant around you. Say yes to the solutions that are being revealed to you. Say yes to the growing opportunities that are showing up for you. Say yes to the love, happiness, and wholeness growing within you. Mostly, and excitedly, say yes to the blessings surrounding you and keep asking for more. Keep saying yes, and good things will show up for you. Make your request and allow all to come to you. Surrender to the process of receiving, then stay patient with the pace of your progress. Open yourself to the possibilities of how it can happen. Take inspired action toward what you want.

April 21

I am Divinely protected and supported.

Today is a day of miracles because you are grounding yourself with gratitude. Be thankful for the experiences that redirected you to new possibilities. Appreciate the cleared paths that made it easy for you to progress towards more. Love that you have released the harmful habits and are on the way to your biggest wins. Use where you want to go as your motivation for more. Celebrate what you have done and where you are. Keep moving forward, and don't look back. Never take your eyes off where you are heading. Say thank you for the "no," acknowledge the "yes," and get ready for better than you can imagine. You are being blessed and Divinely protected.

April 22

I am attracting what I am creating.

Take a moment to reflect on your progress. This is not to live in the past but to acknowledge your tremendous growth and strength. You have worked diligently to improve yourself and your situation; that should be celebrated. Be grateful you are not who you used to be, and your abilities helped you flourish. Keep finding reasons to be happy with the life you have. Embrace the good things unfolding for you. Be grateful for every blessing, big and small. The more you appreciate the now, the more you can build for the future. Honor your progress and keep trusting the process. You are becoming what you are creating. Cheers to your success!

April 23

I am loving my life.

Don't get distracted wanting more and forget to be grateful for what you already have. Overcoming loss and developing gratitude are two of the most challenging lessons in life. Believe that every experience is necessary to your evolution into who you want to become. Sometimes the thing you think is a loss is a clearing to bigger blessings. Life is always giving you clarity from confusion. Learn to appreciate where you have been as you work on where you want to be. Without struggle, you would not be equipped to find what you need to thrive. No matter where you are on your journey, your attitude of gratitude makes a significant difference in your ability to create more. Love your life, and life will love you back.

April 24

I am creating my success.

Instead of allowing your experiences to challenge your confidence, resist giving up. The more you are thankful for your lessons, the more you will receive blessings. Experiences remove the self-imposed limits you were taught. Don't make the tutorial harder by staying stuck in the old way. Make it easy; embrace the knowledge that is leveling you up to more. Today reclaim your power to create better by using what you know. You have been equipped to overcome this exact moment. You already have the strength, abilities, and resources around you required for the win. Decide that no matter what comes your way, you will push past it to the victory line. Miracles happen when you create success from your stumbles. You've got this!

April 25

I am pushing forward and building bigger.

Living your best life requires you to work on being your best self. Being your best self is not about resisting what is unfolding but embracing your ability to choose. You control how you respond; that is where your power to thrive originates. Yes, life happens, but how you create from the setback leads to the setup. There will always be obstacles; only you can shape what happens after. You can retreat and stay small or push forward and build your big. Trust that what you are going through is working in your favor. Try not to question why this is happening to you; instead, focus on what is trying to emerge for you. Be determined to win with what you are given. No matter how things get, better days will happen.

April 26

I am a human Be-ing.

Only you can take charge of creating your love, peace, and satisfaction from within. Nothing outside of you will make you fulfilled unless you decide to find it within. No amount of money, job, or relationship can bring you real joy unless you cultivate it from your soul. Happiness and contentment are emotions you feel and are great tools to help manifest what you want. Manifestation happens when how you feel aligns with what you want. If you feel good about your desires, they will materialize faster. Focus on 'Be-ing' what you want and release the 'Do-ing.' You must be a 'human-being' before you are a happy 'human-doing.' Learn to become before you welcome.

April 27

I am practicing patience while preparing for more.

Obstacles appear as blocks, but they are blessings Divinely sent to redirect you to the easiest path to your happiness. Before you get impatient, doubtful, or discouraged, remember you asked for more, and you are being guided there. You might not immediately attract what you want, but you always attract the lessons that get you there. What you are experiencing is the process that enables you to evolve. What challenges you will change you and bless you with everything you ever wanted. Life is always trying to give you what you ask for. Practicing patience is necessary to prepare you for bigger. Remember, what's yours is yours, and it cannot be denied.

April 28

I am dedicated to my well-being.

If you are dedicated to your work on your well-being, you know your wishes will manifest. Despite the stormy weather, do not abandon the ship. Don't give up when what you want does not materialize in the timeframe you expected. Focus on your progress. Hold on and ride it out to your success. You were not brought this far to be left unsupported or unfulfilled. You are ready to receive what you prayed about. Don't give up right before your miracle manifests. If you are being made to wait, trust you are being transformed to receive more than you can imagine possible. Remember, waiting is preparation for more winning. Keep going; you will get what you want soon.

April 29

I am welcoming my win.

What you want shows up when you are ready. When you ask for blessings, you must be willing to do what is necessary to prepare for them. Don't get impatient; figure out where the work must be done. Readiness can be changed mindset, improved behavior, or commitment to consistent action. The moment you release the worry about the when you begin to welcome the win. Nothing can delay the victory you have been working towards. Everyone can make the changes they want, but it takes tenacity to have the faith to wait. Patience is important to the process. Stop questioning the "Yes." Let go of the doubt and keep doing; you already got your answer. This is your confirmation from the Universe that it is done!

April 30

I am creating a way through.

Everything is always working out for you. Tell yourself this every time you feel discouraged or doubtful. You must trust that you are not where you are today by chance but by grace. All your experiences are necessary for your betterment and are part of a bigger plan to transform you. The faster you learn to see the purpose of all you go through, the more efficiently you respond and create the experiences you want to have. Become the creator of what you want to manifest. Ask, then concentrate on who you need to be to get there. The Universe's job is to work out the details and bring it all to you. Remember, you are the point of attraction. Become the magnet for all your desires and what you want will flow to you with ease.

May 01

I am rejoicing and declaring I have everything I need.

This May, I am finding joy through acknowledging my blessings. I am thankful for what has gone, and I am hopeful for what is yet to come. As I leave the past behind, I am expecting success, abundance, and real love. I am expecting support, opened doors, and unlimited possibilities to keep thriving. I am confidently embracing who I am and the unlimited possibilities for my life. I am confident that the blessings coming to me are for my highest good. I am hopeful that my paths are cleared, my miracles are manifesting, and that things are working out for me. I am celebrating the abundant opportunities for success that are showing up for me. Life is good to me.

May 02

I am growing in gratitude.

Sometimes what holds you back is your belief that 'something' is holding you back. Nothing is in your way. As you read this, trust the Universe is sending you everything you need to thrive. Be proud of your role in your change. You have made sure you are not repeating old tricks attempting to get new results. You have worked diligently to improve yourself and your circumstances. Keep loving yourself enough to give yourself everything you ever wanted. Know that while you work on yourself, more mistakes will be made, which is okay. Don't try to skip them; conquer them and use them. Bring all of you and use it to build a good life. Show up for your happiness by working today for what you want tomorrow. Today honor your progress.

May 03

I am feeding my faith.

You grow what you fertilize. If you keep feeding your fear, you will keep cultivating struggle and resistance. Remember, you are a powerful creator who can transform your life through your responses and choices. Every moment you stay stuck in doubt delays what you want to achieve. Don't let your self-created limits keep you from your unlimited possibilities. Faith is the feeling; allowing is the action needed to make your desires manifest. When you trust things will work out in your favor, the only work for you to do is to let it in. Only you can work on what is blocking your blessings and allow your happiness in. Feed your faith, and you will manifest miracles. You are what you expect. Expect good things will happen for you in all ways.

May 04

I am actively creating more.

You cannot be heard if you don't speak up. You cannot harvest if you don't plant. You cannot heal if you don't address your hurt. You cannot find peace if you don't get still enough to listen for Divine direction. Whatever you are searching for, it takes changed behavior to achieve it. Get out of your way by releasing the limiting habits, negative beliefs, or doubt about what you deserve. To find happiness, you must move past your hurt and acknowledge what brings you peace. To thrive, you must push past your limits and focus on your worth. Trust you are transforming for the better. The Universe wants you to have what you lack. Life won't get better unless you actively create more. You have what it takes to make your change.

May 05

I am always given what I need to thrive.

Sometimes it is easy to get discouraged by what you lack and never consider what you were saved from. What you think you have lost was a lesson in resilience, planting, patience, and harvesting. You have to understand how to live without, to appreciate what you have. Struggle does not happen because you don't know how to thrive; it occurs when you are being pushed to unleash your full potential. In learning what you are capable of overcoming, you understand what you are capable of creating. Today appreciate where you are starting and that you are standing. Be thankful for the blessings you received from the challenges you experienced. Stay grateful, focused, and keep pushing forward.

May 06

I am standing proudly in my power.

Without the broken heart, you would not have broken free from what was holding you back. Without the struggle, you would never know your real strength. Without the lack, you would not have leveled up to more. Without the doubt, you would not have found your truth. The times you got knocked down taught you how to find and develop your stance. You never fall because you are a failure, you are only challenged to climb higher than you believe possible. You passed every test you have faced, and you are still standing. Take this moment to marvel at how extraordinary that position is. Today stand proudly in your position of power. You are amazing, trust that.

May 07

I am faithful to the future I deserve.

Yes, it is hard to make a change after being challenged. Yes, it is tiring to move forward after you have been blocked. Yes, it isn't easy to let go when you want to hold on. But not working on finding the happiness you deserve is leaving you disappointed. Move past wasting time stuck in fear and have faith in the future you deserve. Only you can put effort into your happiness. When you want to find love, start with loving all of you. When you want more support, believe in your abilities. When you want peace, align with Source. When you want to develop courage, put aside past fears. When you want to move forward, get over yesterday. When you want abundance, believe in more.

May 08

I am living life to the fullest.

Everything you ask for is born from a place of wanting happiness. Real love is rare; cherish it with gratitude. Anger is destructive; forgive, let go and leave it in the past. Fear is limiting; face it and move forward to your victory. Worthiness is your birthright, value who you are, and reclaim it at any moment. Memories are precious; cherish them forever in your heart. Only you can make the change to create what you want. If you ask for love, practice compassion. If you asked for abundance, use your gifts to create more. If you asked for peace, respond before you react. You create change when you make mindful, consistent choices, that align with what you want to manifest. Life is short; don't forget to live it to the fullest.

May 09

I am trusting my harvest will happen soon.

When you feel like you are down to nothing, the Universe is silently up to something. If you don't currently see the miracle, trust your magic will manifest at the right time. The answers you seek have already been delivered. Take a moment to inventory what is showing up for you and find the blessings unfolding. Remember, solutions can be given as seeds, and the fruit is the last thing to appear. Plant, fertilize them, and refrain from digging them up with doubt. Stay hopeful and expectant. Stay patient and allow them time to grow. Everything has a season and a reason, even when it's time for your harvest. Trust what you have planted is growing.

May 10

I am expecting all my dreams to come true.

Start every day with positive thoughts of what you want to create in your life. Request what you want and allow it to unfold. You don't need to know the when, where, why, or even how it will happen. You just need to ask for it, believe in it, show up, and do your part to welcome it. Trust the actions you are taking; the inner work you are doing will be paying off soon. You have what it takes; keep going. Don't doubt your abilities or the timing of your results; have faith it is done, and it will be delivered. Time has no power when you are patient and believe in your purpose. Trust in Divine timing. Everything happens as it should when it should.

May 11

I am always given what I need right on time.

Today appreciate where you are standing. Be thankful for the blessings you have and the challenges you never experienced. Stay grateful, focused, and keep pushing forward. Trust your prayers are being answered. You have more miracles manifesting than you can imagine. Remember, successful manifestations begin as thoughts then transform into your reality through inspired actions. Everything you experience helps you create. You are always learning, growing, and expanding. This process is your evolution into more. Be confident in what you do, and it will create what you want. Let the desire for change lead you forward. Trust that when you ask, it is Divinely given.

May 12

I am embracing who I am and who I can become.

Life is always trying to give you what you need, not what you think you want. When a door closes, be grateful, that was not your way. Blocks don't mean you were denied; they are signals to look for the opening to more. Don't get so focused on the closed door you miss your destined opportunity. Pay attention; the path to what you want is being revealed. Release the how and embrace the possibilities. What you asked for is always given; your openness to the way makes it easier. Allow forces more significant than you to support and guide you there. What is yours can never be denied; it is ready and waiting for you to enter. Embrace where you are; it is where you are supposed to be.

May 13

I am choosing happiness.

Mind-FULL-ness is the peace of mind to stay present to empower yourself to move forward. The need to control how life should unfold is where disappointment can set in. Don’t get busy looking outside of yourself for inspiration and forget to look within. Only you can decide on what you want for your life. If you want to create change, you have to do the things that push you from your comfort zones. Comfort is counterproductive to creativity. You are a powerful creator with the ability to expand your life into anything you want. You already have everything you need within to do this. Don't let the illusion of the impossible keep you from your possible. Make the time daily to connect with what inspires you to grow. Happiness is a feeling, not a destination.

May 14

I am mastering what I need to win.

Some dreams unfold easily, and others require a lot more inner work before they manifest. The areas that labor you the most are the ones that bring the most significant rewards. Education has its levels, and so does life. To live better, sometimes you must learn better. You are never tested on what you know; you are pushed to master what you need to win. Don't get distracted by the lesson and ignore what the final exam is trying to bring into your life. Trust the process because life always wants you to succeed. If needed, Source will move mountains to give you all that you've requested. Stop resisting the test. Allow your dreams to manifest in ways you could not have imagined.

May 15

I am doing a great job with my happiness.

Time always reveals what's yours. Don't let your impatience signal to the Universe that you don't believe in what you deserve. Trust that bigger is coming and get ready for it. What's meant for you is flowing to you, and what was never yours is fleeing from you. Ask yourself what you need to do today to get prepared for your more tomorrow. When everything falls into place, you will be amazed at how worthy the Universe thinks you are. Use the moon as your greatest inspiration and remember that you don't always have to be whole to win. Keep showing up on your tough days, best days, and in-between days. You have what it takes to shine bigger and brighter.

May 16

I am releasing with grace and welcoming with gratitude.

Sometimes reality can be challenging. Trust you can transform your life by asking for mental clarity to overcome what holds you back. Releasing the limits, healing the pain, and forgiving the unforgettable is necessary for stepping away before you step forward. Find your way by shifting from surviving to thriving. Start with accepting that your experiences do not define you; they only reveal the true you. The Universe is continually working to remove the obstacles you cannot see. Be grateful for your progress while you work on where you want to go. It is possible to believe in your dreams and not be clear about how you will get there. Don't let the unknown keep you from going after your all.

May 17

I am supporting my dreams.

Everyone can have moments where they lack confidence or feel like giving up on pursuing what they deserve. Those are the days that define your persistence. Don't let one day deter you from seeing your better days. Release the worry about how any day goes. Remember, you can always try again tomorrow. No one is coming to save you or bring you happiness. You have to do that for yourself. Yes, past trauma can lead most to a life of survival, but what keeps you from thriving is the self-imposed limits you created because of pain. Today connect with the infinite possibilities of your potential. Reclaim your worth by acknowledging you are capable of having all you desire. Love, abundance, and success are already within you. Confidently be yourself; you are amazing.

May 18

I am proud of who I am becoming.

If you don't move past what hurts you, it will be challenging to move to what will heal you. Don't be ashamed to work on you; everyone has something they are trying to get over. Healing helps you to bridge the gap between affliction so that you can create affection for yourself. When you focus on the hurt, you cannot focus on the healing. Self-love and forgiveness are necessary for finding the peace you seek. Free yourself by connecting with who you are without the pain. There are bigger beautiful parts of you that you tend to forget. Today find them and highlight them. You are remarkable and resilient; never forget that. You are already blessed. Be at peace, my friend.

May 19

I am expecting a great day today.

Even though you cannot see it, trust that your best days are yet to come. Many people train themselves to look at what is rather than imagine what could be. Focusing on your present circumstances can undermine your confidence to create your possibilities. Begin with imagining better is possible, and you are capable of producing it. Find yourself, and you will always find your way. Let the greatness in you radiate despite what you face. Accept the now, release the past, and love yourself enough to focus on your future. Don't ever doubt your ability to accomplish your dreams. Rejoice in the blessings and Divine miracles coming your way. Purpose attracts possibilities, and gratitude attracts greatness. You are destined for great things.

May 20

I am balancing my energy.

From the instant you create a desire to the moment it materializes, there is momentum that needs to build. Everything you seek requires time to greet you where you are trying to meet it. It is your job to step up and align with your needs to bring them closer to you. When you get impatient and doubt the probability of your dreams happening, you only delay the manifestation. Let go of the worry and stress that comes with waiting on things to manifest. Focus on the peace of knowing it will happen, rather than the pace it is happening. Life has to go slow at times, so you can prepare for when it starts to go fast. Appreciate the beauty in the pace and give thanks for the peace. You create your reality when you trust in its possibility. Enjoy being in standby mode before go mode.

May 21

I am creating my miracles from a place of love.

You can reap what you sow; therefore, setting the right intention for your life is important. When you make your decisions, create them from a good mental space. Try not to make them from limiting emotions like hurt, regret, or impatience. Getting clear about how you want to feel will help you make better decisions. When you exercise your power of choice, you make your life easier. Every day set out to feel good and allow your choices to reflect the pursuit of those feelings. Actively working on your emotional well-being gives you the power to create constructive changes. Before you act, set the right intentions to produce positivity. When peace and gratitude become a priority, your happiness becomes a natural state of being.

May 22

I am making room for more.

When you woke up and asked the Universe for more abundance, love, peace, success, or happiness, have faith you already got your answer. Sometimes you think the response was no, hold, or be patient, but it is always "Trust. It is done." Remember, when you ask, you will always get the answer for you to make room for more. Your job is to focus on clearing the blocks and preparing for becoming and receiving. Keep praying for the grace and dignity to release what you do not need. Ask for the ability to clean and clear without creating another mess. Allow what needs to be eliminated to be put aside with poise. Make room for your plenty by welcoming unlimited prosperity and possibilities. Stay grateful for the good things flowing to you.

May 23

I am always writing a beautiful story for my life.

Everywhere you have been, prepared you for where you are going. You are born with a purpose, and it is your choice to pursue it. Every chapter of your life is teaching you your capacity to love, evolve, and create. If you need to forgive someone, consider forgiveness your blessing, not theirs. This is the only way to repair and release energetic connections binding you to hurt that holds you in the past. Yesterday is gone; resist replaying the chapter. Healing takes time, but it will unburden your soul. Focus on your possibilities and celebrate your commitment to your happiness. You can empower yourself to create a new story. Trust you are always doing the best you can and be self-compassionate.

May 24

I am doing a great job.

Who you are on the inside is important to what you can create in your outer world. If you don't feel self-love, true love can miss you. If you don't have faith, fear will influence you. If you don't believe you are worthy of all, scarcity will follow you. Focus on who you need to be to live the life you want to welcome. Most importantly, don't judge yourself while you try. Remember, you are continually growing and expanding your preferences. Be self-compassionate and trust you are doing the best you can as you navigate through. Find your confidence, stay strong, and have faith that your experiences are needed to transform you into your best self. Growth can bend you, stretch you, but it will never break you; it builds you into a better version. Keep going; you've got this.

May 25

I am stepping into my greatness.

Every stumble, step back or step up works in your favor. Everything you go through helps you sift, sort, and discern how to create more of what you want. When you think the Universe has left you to fight and figure it out on your own, something will show up to reveal you were always supported. Trust life is working for you, with you, and ahead of you. Don't ever doubt your talents; use them to accomplish your dreams. Work on who you are and what you want will fall into place. Rejoice in the blessings and Divine miracles coming your way. Purpose attracts possibilities, and gratitude attracts greatness. Now is the time to make your change. Have faith, obstacles are being cleared, bridges are being built, and doors are being opened. Keep going. Trust the Universe has your back.

May 26

I am embracing new opportunities.

Letting go hurts when you focus on holding on. Gently release your hold on the old and welcome the freedom it will give you to receive more. Embrace the new opportunities being presented. Growing pains are inevitable, however, staying stuck in the suffering after the experience is optional. When you keep living in the hurt, you cannot focus on your future's unlimited possibilities. Doors are often closed to redirect you to true happiness. Remember, you never have to fight to keep what is already yours. Do yourself a favor and take control of where your mental energy goes. Only you can determine what makes you happy enough to thrive. Free yourself from the past and make room to create the life you want to welcome.

May 27

I am pushing forward to my victory.

The experiences you face were designed to uncover the real you. You don't know what you possess until who you are is questioned. You don't see what you can endure until the pressure is applied. You don't know what courage you can muster until you have been under fire. Your value never changes based on what you go through; it only improves. The grape never complains it's being crushed; it becomes wine. A diamond shines because of the pressure that forms it. Even seeds grow in the dark before they see the light. Consider where you are as a powerful place of transformation. Trust the process, crush your goals, press on, shine, and bloom. The best is yet to come. Push forward to your victory.

May 28

I am receiving clear direction in my life.

When you sit to pray with gratitude, take it a step further by welcoming guidance and solutions. Have a conversation with God today by getting still enough to listen. Move past asking for deliverance and open a channel to receive direction. Prayer is when you ask, and meditation is when you are answered. Remember, your prayers are ALL ways being answered. The mental state you asked from can determine the answer you get. If the reply is yes, you did the work to believe and receive. If the response is no, don't despair. You are only being guided to release the limiting mindset about what you deserve. All answers are necessary for your advancement to more.

May 29

I am welcoming an abundant harvest.

How do you work with your rain? Are you using it to make your future grow, or are you holding on to it to justify continued discontentment? Move towards your healing by not letting the past influence your current experiences. It is gone; release it, forgive it, and accept your responsibility to create your sunshine. Remember, storms always end. No matter how overcast it looks right now, believe in the beautiful blue skies above. Whatever you may be experiencing, focus on the promise, not your planting. Clouds bring the rain that nourishes and creates life. Rain taught you resilience and the patience to welcome your harvest. Thank every drop.

May 30

I am unlimited potential.

Believe that every experience is designed to help you find your true self - the part of you closest to Source. It is not the whisper that says you cannot, but the voice that says you can. It is the part of you that recognizes that your creativity has unlimited potential. Embrace it by understanding you have the power to produce the life you want. When the Universe is for you, nothing can be against you. Remember, Source knows what you want and is always guiding you there; even a no is working in your favor. What you want is on the way and delivered when you are truly ready to receive it. Trust the process that gets you what you desire. Blessings are never late; you are impatient. You weren't given a vision or brought this far to fail. Have faith you will fly!

May 31

I am flourishing.

When you give your soul what it needs, you find inspiration to keep thriving. When you make positive feelings your priority, you align with your best self. When you feel stuck, you are disconnected from your needs and who you are. Life is always showing you how to make your way back to you. You were created as a beautiful and unique soul with a specific path. Do not allow anything to overshadow who you are and what you are capable of achieving. Only you can give yourself what you need to flourish on your journey. You have more miracles manifesting than you acknowledge. Find it by focusing on what makes you happy. Trust you are already moving forward. Have faith; everything is always working out for you.

June 01

I am more.

This June, I am entering a season of more. More connections. More peace. More tolerance. More security. More freedom. More love. More compassion. More joy. More abundance. More spiritual alignment. More clarity. More support. More well-being. More upliftment. More grace. More discernment. More laughter. More dancing. More inspiration. More delight in my days. More acceptance. More Divine timing. More patience. More Divine guidance. More spontaneous blessings. More opened doors. More cleared paths. More creativity. More miracles. More satisfaction. More goodness. More me.

June 02

I am present and finding peace.

It's not the times you decide to fight; it's the times you choose to surrender to the freedom that healing will bring. Forgive yourself and others. This does not make you weak; it sets you free. Release yourself from carrying the pain by being present enough to find what makes you happy. Anything that negatively impacts your heart, or your life, is not easy to move past. Change is always hard in the beginning, a big mess in the middle, but miraculously comes together at the end. No matter how many times you have to start over, give yourself grace for trying. Keep pushing through all the stages as best as you can. Focus on the good feelings you want to feel. Stay in the moment to find the peace that is present. The journey of maintaining your well-being is worth it.

June 03

I am clear about what I want to welcome.

Consider your intentions the fuel behind your desires; they are the power source to your miracles. Defining what's at the heart of what you want helps you identify it before it arrives. Before you receive, you must set intentions with clarity and from a good mental space. If you asked for love, notice when kindness is given. If you asked for abundance, use your gifts to create more. If you asked for peace, choose how you respond. Always be open to how you receive your answers. Love, prosperity, and peace can show up in multiple ways. Look around; results may already be showing up for you. For example, an abundance of time can help you build a life you love. Trust you are constantly receiving feedback from the Universe.

June 04

I am consistently producing.

Consider yourself the gardener and your dreams a seed that needs planting. As the cultivator, you cannot get impatient or rush the growth process. This will not make it flourish any faster. With time, nurturing, consistent care, and love, you have to believe it will grow into more. Remember, seeds are always given what they need to thrive when they need it. They never have to worry about rain or sunshine. Growth needs time for expansion and transformation. Keep trusting that your planting is consistently producing, even when you do not see it. Give your seed time to push through the dirt and blossom. What is for you always shows up at the right time. Your job is to focus on making the environment optimal for your seed's thriving.

June 05

I am pushing through to my breakthrough.

Bless the struggle you endured; it activated your pursuit of success. Thank the constant pushing forward; it uncovered your strength. Forgive the rejection you received; it revealed your true worth. Embrace the desire you developed for more; it ignited your fire to pursue all. You cannot love who you are and dislike what shaped you. Don't discard the fight to survive; it created your passion for thriving. Remember, happiness isn't discovered when you stay stuck on what is going wrong; it is produced when you do more of what makes things right. Sometimes the problem isn't the problem; it is your approach to the problem. Try focusing on the solution. You already have what it takes to create change.

June 06

I am committed to my happiness.

When life unexpectedly changes, regain control by understanding you have the power to create a new vision. Stop reliving what could have been; focus on the now and what could be. Take the time to heal, focus on what you want, then start creating that. Remember, buildings are built one brick at a time, and your happiness also requires commitment day to day. Today embrace all of you and use it to create more of you. Keep working through and pushing through until your breakthrough. Stop thinking you are not ready to build; you are. You cannot manifest your desires if you doubt your abilities. You owe it to yourself to go after all of your dreams. Just start. You've got this.

June 07

I am flowing in the right direction.

Everything unfolding in your life has a reason and season. Your experiences are only pushing you in the direction of what you prayed for and requested. Struggles set in when you refuse to let go of how you think it should unfold. Release the grip and welcome guidance to get what you want. You can't fix your past, but you can be different today for your tomorrow. Don't allow mistakes to hold you back; find your unique gifts and press forward. Remember, you are continually growing, expanding, and creating change. Be intentional with your happiness. What you want is trying to manifest for you; allow it to happen. Stop fighting to stay small, flow, and grow into your all.

June 08

I am creating good emotions.

Make your positive feelings a priority, and they will help you manage where you are. When you actively focus on how you want to feel, you will find your mental clarity and well-being. Gratitude, hope, or satisfaction with life can fill you up, energize you, and prepare you to cater to challenges and others. Despite how your day unfolds, using good emotions can keep you grounded. Encourage yourself with positive statements about your progress. Use affirmations to help you reprogram your mind from habitually negative thinking and refocus on positive possibilities. Count your blessings constantly. Whatever you do, concentrate on the activities that bring you peace. Caring for your well-being is not selfish; it is self-first.

June 09

I am trusting my path forward.

You thrive when you learn to appreciate your lessons, not resist them. Everything you overcame prepared you for your purpose and is valuable to your victory. Both trials and triumphs teach you what and who is important to your well-being. You may lose people and things along the way, but you always collect the skills necessary for evolution. Remember, it is who you become after your experiences that create your story. You must know down to recognize up. You must know sadness before you choose to fight to become happy. You must understand what lack feels like before you pursue your abundance. How else will you learn to define what is important to you? Trust the process that helps clear your path, develop your skills, and guide you to fulfill your purpose.

June 10

I am open to receiving all good things.

Answers to prayers can come in many forms, even learning to let go of what holds you back. Be good at asking and even better at receiving. Sometimes what you desire does not arrive in the way you expect or the timeframe you want, and that is okay. Pay attention to what is showing up; it is the only way to recognize the abundant blessings surrounding you. Allow where you are and what you have to be enough. Trust what you want will materialize. Life is about doing your best on the ride, learning along the way, and not waiting for the arrival. That is where it all ends. The Universe is ALL-ways working to give you what you asked for. Keep believing in your prayers.

June 11

I am pursuing the highest vision for my life.

When what you do isn't getting you to where you want to go, stop holding on to what you cannot control and focus on what you can - you and your responses. When you ask for more, the quietest part of you will never forget that you are worthy of receiving all and will guide you there. Change can be challenging, but to create more, you have to transform into more. Only you can pursue the highest vision for your life. Make the most of your journey, pray for discernment and patience to recognize that you are being guided through it all. Trust you are on your way to more. Make the change easier by releasing your resistance. Have faith everything is moving you closer to your desires.

June 12

I am trusting things are working out for me.

Uncertainty about your future will occasionally happen. It is okay when you don't have all the answers or know where you are going or doing. Focus on what you do know and let that work in your favor. It’s human nature to dread letting go or stepping into the unknown, but you must make the leap to get the reward. Before you know it, you will regain your clarity, paths will be cleared, and you will find your way through to the other side. Remember, you have what it takes to create change. Find your courage to move forward by trusting it is all part of a bigger plan. That first step may not be your most decisive or most straightforward move, but it is a necessary action if you want to succeed.

June 13

I am infinite potential.

You don't get where you want by remaining who you are. When you let go of the beliefs that limit you, you allow success beyond what you can perceive for yourself to become available to you. The unknown should never keep you from your happiness. Start by holding yourself accountable for the role you play in the creation of the life you want. Continue to work on your healing by committing to what makes your soul happy. Trust that everything you do is making room for the triumph you desire. Keep moving forward the best you can. Things are continually working out for you because you have infinite potential. Stop doing things your way; surrender to a new way. A way that understands that you are the creator born to create. Nothing you do is ever wasted.

June 14

I am deserving of more.

Don't get distracted by the lack and miss the magnitude of what is trying to make its way into your life. Sometimes you don't get what you want, not because you don't deserve it, but because you deserve more. You have to believe in more to receive more. When you doubt whether you can attain true happiness, remember the improvements you made, the mindset you changed, the abundance you created from nothing, the mountains you conquered, the stormy seas you navigated through, the wins you fought for, and the progress you pushed past despite the struggle. Rejection, resilience, receiving, and redemption are all seasons that have reasons. They are necessary for your journey. Blessings always follow challenges and changes. Trust in Divine timing.

June 15

I am making room for my more.

Continue to work on your forgiveness and healing by finding what fills your heart and balances your soul. Choices made with self-compassion make moving past mistakes more manageable. Don't get stuck on a missed step; keep thanking and trusting in your possibilities. Forgive those who did not know how to love you; they taught you self-love. Forgive those who did not know how to treat you as you deserve; they showed you self-care. Forgive those who did not believe in your dreams; they pushed you to go forward and self-motivate. Forgive those who did not know how to support you; they helped you develop your inner strength. Forgive and make room in your soul to become the best version of yourself. Forgiveness unburdens your soul.

June 16

I am being redirected to more.

When you create from a shortage mindset, unstable foundations are built. They will eventually crumble to reveal your full potential. Sometimes what you think you want isn't what you need. Be grateful that what you thought you wanted never materialized. Trust you were being protected and redirected toward more. Occasionally you are blocked before better is brought to you. Keep practicing gratitude for what you were saved from and what you are given. What is yours can never be taken away. Slow down and build from a better place by believing your miracles are already done. Today, love where you are, who you are, and where you are going. Sometimes what you wanted is too small for the significance of what you are capable of creating for your life.

June 17

I am empowering myself to fly.

It is important to understand that every experience is essential to the creation of your happiness. Struggle builds strength, challenges reveal clarity, and patience develops your peace. Don't discount the value of anything; it defines you. The faster you learn to recognize the reason for the challenge, the quicker you can course correct. Everything that drowns you teaches you how to swim. Everything that challenges you cultivates your strength. Everything that blocks you pushes you to persevere. Everything that delays you develops your endurance. Everything that scares you builds your bravery. Everything that stops your progress shows you how to flow. Everything that leaves you frees you to level up. Everything that made you fall empowered you to fly high. Fly, my friend, fly.

June 18

I am staying positive and hopeful.

How you think affects how you live. Today push aside any negative thoughts that keep you from taking action. Negative experiences show the dark areas that need a positive light. If you think you are lacking, look at what you have. If you think you don't have what it takes, look at what you have achieved. If you constantly worry, recognize you are capable of creating solutions. Every thought you think has two sides, what is wanted and what isn't wanted. It is your choice to focus on what is wanted. Remember, life is always trying to give you what you need, and sometimes it is not in the way you expected. Always trust things are working out for you. Focus on the good showing up.

June 19

I am growing and thriving.

Blessings never look like the prayers you prayed. When you asked for love or abundance, you probably already got your answer. Today, take another look at your life and understand the power and potential of what you have been given. The blessing may appear to be small, but with nurturing, it will turn into something significant. A healer will experience hurt before they can heal. A leader will get lost before they can find their way. Experiences of lack will push you to build abundance. Past failures will produce your drive to succeed. Trust you will always be shown the way back to your best self. Whatever phase you are in, you have the power to decide what you create next. Blessings are sent to grow you while you grow them. Trust the process that brings more.

June 20

I am surrendering to the process.

If you trust the Universe like you claim you do, why do you doubt your manifestations? Stop being impatient by questioning the timing of what you deserve. Be grateful that life offers second chances, fresh starts, and unlimited opportunities to change course. Life wants to give you everything you desire and more. Your path is already cleared. Your love is already aligned. Your abundance is already accumulated. Your success is already set. Your door is already opened. Your support is already showing up. Your peace is already produced. Your health is already improving. Your worry is already washing away. Your dreams are already being delivered. Surrender to the process that produces the results you want.

June 21

I am loving all of me.

The parts you are ashamed of showed you how strong you are. The parts you want to bury taught you how to push through dirt and grow. The parts that broke you opened allowed you to let more in. The parts that you want to keep in the dark will make you shine. The parts you need to forgive will empower you to forge forward. The parts that created limits are showing you have to level up. The parts that kept you small is showing you how to create your big. The parts that made you feel unworthy showed you how invaluable you are. Every piece of you makes you complete. Remember, you become what you can dream possible. Embrace who you are and use what you know to produce what you want. Learn to love all of you, and you will thrive. You are already whole. Use it all to create your world.

June 22

I am ready for more than I can imagine for myself.

Be receptive to more than you can imagine for yourself. Where you are standing isn't the highest you can climb. Start going for your all by gracefully letting go of what cannot be taken to the top. Stay devoted to your happiness, and you will create miracles. Stay committed to what feeds your soul, and you will achieve success. Stay patient on your path, and you will develop perseverance. Stay faithful to the vision of your future, and it will be fruitful. Stay focused on feeling good, and you will improve your well-being. Stay loving who you are, and you will align with the people that reflect your self-love. Stay planting, and you will harvest. Stay climbing; every step is creating your victory.

June 23

I am pushing forward.

If you feel exhausted from pushing through the dirt, understand your frustration might arise from going in the wrong direction. Stop pushing backward; start pushing forward. Leave what burdens you behind, release it, and lighten your load. You cannot advance with hands full of hurt. Give the past no power in the present. Let it all go and change what you carry. Choose to hold love for who you are in your heart. Choose to hold your accomplishments at the forefront of your mind. Choose to hold your limitless potential and the highest vision for your life as your primary focus. Choose to hold your happiness as a priority for your choices. Positivity will help you push forward. Remember, only you can choose your well-being.

June 24

I am blessed.

Today, be grateful for what you have and what you have never gone through and Divinely protected from. Acknowledge that whatever path you were given, you found your way. That is a significant accomplishment that is worthy of recognition. You are the one that stepped up and out in faith to create your change. You are not standing where you are by chance; you are thriving by choice. Appreciate your ability to overcome and always keep forging forward. Bless what is left and stay thankful and focused on what's showing up. The Universe is always giving you feedback on your dedication to your happiness. You are doing a great job manifesting the life you want. You are blessed. Trust more is still to come.

June 25

I am taking it one day at a time.

The areas that require more focus from you teach you how to overcome what is mentally blocking you. If you are doubting what you are doing, work on improving how you are feeling. Pursuing activities that make you happy will help you shift to positive emotions. When you feel good, your self-esteem builds. The better you feel about who you are, the more dedicated you become to creating goals and crushing them. You owe it to yourself to go after your happiness. Just start, stay present, and take it one day at a time, one choice at a time. Remember, success is a series of continual steps; no matter how solid or shaky they are, trust they all make up a fulfilling and victorious journey. Find what feeds your soul daily, and you will find your way.

June 26

I am feeding and fueling my mind with positivity.

Are you excitedly preparing for love, success, healing, peace, or abundance to manifest? Or are you spending your time questioning if happiness is even possible for you? Whatever you doubt, you cannot manifest. Put aside your fear and feed yourself encouragement, hope, and positivity. Your body is listening to your mind. Remember, you are what you expect. Use your words to build your confidence in what you can achieve. The most powerful words to help with belief begin with "I am." Let your affirmation statement today be about what you desire in your life tomorrow. Say it, believe it, prepare to receive it, then be guided to create it. You already have what it takes to succeed.

June 27

I am trusting the pieces are falling into place.

When things feel like they aren't going anywhere or appear to progress slowly, trust the pieces will silently fall into place. The Universe has your back. Remember, when you ask, it is Divinely given. There are always parts of a plan being positioned that don't need your input or effort. Just sit back and be amazed at how well it all comes together. Stick to the decisions you have made to pursue your happiness; they will pay off soon. What you want will happen right on time. For all you know, you might be one moment away from it materializing. Expect the best, always. You deserve to have whatever you are working on building. If you planted it, started it, or were guided to it, trust you will finish it and have it.

June 28

I am making my happiness happen.

Satisfaction and gratitude are powerful emotions that are essential to your thriving. How you choose to feel can have healing and magnifying powers. Focus on the good in your life. Use appreciation to amplify your ability to attract more abundance and well-being. The challenge is not what you do, but who you decide to become. Only you can transform your hopefulness into the happiness you want from life. Only you can elevate your moments of joy into a lifetime of ecstasy. Only you can use your internal peace to produce harmony living with others. Only you can see that your little is more than plenty to create the life you want. Whatever you desire, your dedication can make it happen.

June 29

I am making every moment count.

Stop giving doubt the ability to hold you back from having what you want. Look at what you have built thus far and remember your why for starting. You created everything you have today. Be proud of your progress. Put all your energy into producing the possibilities you want for yourself. Remember, it only takes one change in mindset, one choice, or one specific action to materialize the significant change you want. All your power lies in your right here and right now. This is the only moment that matters to what you can manifest. Believe you can and allow inspired action to get you there. Make this moment matter. Keep going. Never doubt your ability to create more.

June 30

I am trusting things are changing in my favor.

Endings are always beginnings because the potential for new possibilities is limitless. Remember, you cannot take back what you have asked for, but you can add more details to what you desire. Put everything into crafting every aspect of what you want next, then allow it to transition in a way that works for you and only you. When you exit out of one phase and enter into another, be patient, the process requires time. Life happens differently for everyone. It only takes one moment for everything to unexpectantly manifest. Your persistence to your happiness will pay off soon. Life is about to change in your favor. You don't have anything more to do but trust and get prepared.

July 01

I am aligning with the fullness of who I am.

This July, I welcome alignment with the best within me. I will confidently triumph over all that holds me back from pursuing my success. I will bravely push past my fears and take inspired action to create my future. I will effortlessly release my need to overthink and concentrate on creating solutions. I will use what I have to produce the abundance I want to manifest. I will plant and patiently and excitedly prepare for my harvest. I will continue to have faith in my ability to find clear, focused thoughts that lead me toward my happiness. I will delight daily in the blessings showing up for me. I will use all of who I am to build the highest vision for my life.

July 02

I am proud of my progress.

The Universe knows what you want, what you have asked for, and how far you are from your desires. Every day and every little thing you do is designed to get you there. Trust the process that is taking you exactly where you need to be. Put your energy and time into what you are creating, no matter how far you are from your destination. Don't let the distance travelled distract you from the headway you have made. Stand behind what you are doing with pride. Use your skills to create abundance. Open your heart and allow the healing that enables you to receive more. Push yourself out of your comfort zones and meet the people that will support you and help you move forward. Show up for yourself by believing you are worthy of having everything you desire.

July 03

I am prepared to cross the finish line.

You are doing the work to put yourself and your happiness first. That is not selfish, it is self-first. You are the source of your creation. If it weren't for you, where you are today would not be possible. Yes, your trials might feel significant, but they are strengthening your ability to receive bigger blessings. You will always be sent a challenge that reveals the warrior within you. Trust you will triumph and don't get distracted by the battle. Place your effort on crossing the finish line. Remember, you are a powerful creator; focus on your potential, not the pace. When you concentrate on the promise, you understand the fight always has a purpose. Trust it will all transform into a fruitful future.

July 04

I am trusting things will change in my favor soon.

In the moments you feel disheartened about where you are, find something to be thankful for and use that to encourage your progress. Continue trusting things are already transforming around you. Don't lose momentum because you haven't seen the results you want; believe it will manifest soon. Keep creating the change you desire. Trust all your efforts are producing the outcome you want. Find the surprises and blessings along the way; they are all around you. Life is good to you when you believe it is on your side. Your continued hope is key to your success and happiness. Remember, things are always working out for you. Allow everything to fall into place.

July 05

I am learning what I need to thrive from every moment.

There are days designed for you to rest, recoup, and others for you to forge forward. Your times for rest are not about inactivity, they are necessary to re-energize and refocus. When you get weary, you are being directed to slow before you go. Sometimes you need to stand still before you find what is required to keep stepping forward. Concentrate on doing the best you can right now, and you will empower yourself for the next. What you do today can determine the quality of your efforts tomorrow. Learn to understand what you need daily. Take the time to tune in and connect with your desires. Every day has a purpose for the steps on your path. Thriving occasionally requires a timeout.

July 06

I am making great improvements in my life.

Yes, it may seem like you are doing the same things repeatedly, or your efforts feel monotonous, but trust you are making improvements. Who you are right now isn't the same person that started the journey. Acknowledge the change you created within yourself and the progress you built in your life. At this instant, trust support is aligning, paths are being prepared, and things are moving right where you need them to be. Use this moment to look at how your life has been enriched and give yourself credit for doing it. You are creating what you want. Remember, progress requires momentum and needs time to pick up the pace. Believe in the beautiful life you are building. You've got this.

July 07

I am believing in the possibilities of my plenty.

Give yourself more credit for what you are creating. You have repeatedly gotten up after being knocked down. You pushed forward without knowing where you were going. You made breakthroughs from breakdowns and breakups. You leveled up despite the limiting mindset that needed to be released. You found your wholeness by acknowledging your true worth. Yes, you have more to do, but stop and look at what you have produced thus far. Keep going and believing in the possibilities of your plenty. With everything you are doing, you have to trust the next natural stage will be better. You are already on your way to more.

July 08

I am thankful for my daily provisions.

Today pray with faith and gratitude for the fruitful future that is already prepared for you. Today invite success and support for where you are going. Today find the paths that are cleared ahead of you. Today appreciate the healing that is revealing your wholeness. Today welcome the abundance that is already surrounding you. Today celebrate what you are doing to produce the life you want. Today embrace the goodness in your life and work to create more of what you desire. Every day is a good day to love the life you are living. Say thank you for your daily provisions and manifested blessings as if they are guaranteed. Believe your miracles will happen, and don't give up now.

July 09

I am finding my clarity.

What is under the surface is more important than what you see up top. How you feel on the inside is manifesting your life on the outside. Your prayers may be delayed because your internal signals to the Universe are different from what you said you wanted. The Universe does not hear your words; it hears your heart. When you pray for love, work on feeling your self-love. When you pray for prosperity, work on filling yourself up with contentment for what you have. When you pray for peace, work on your inner security. Get clear on what you want, and don't let hidden whispers overshadow your wishes. What you believe is what you become. Setting intentions from a good emotional state will produce the results you want to see manifest.

July 10

I am proud of my progress.

Your life is changing because you changed. Every step you took improved your self-confidence. You showed yourself how capable you are of building better. You shifted from your comfort zones and embraced your personal power to produce more. You did what needed to be done to create your inner peace and prosperity. You acknowledged your purpose, and you stuck to the path. Be proud of yourself and your progress. You may not be where you want to be, but you are intentionally making your way there. Keep trusting in your ability to succeed. Remember, starting any transformation can seem challenging, but finishing it will be extremely rewarding. Everything is already working out in your favor. Take time to celebrate your commitment to your happiness.

July 11

I am being and staying positive.

Today be grateful for the blessings you are experiencing. Be inspired by your growth and your continued focus on what you want to welcome. Be thankful for the transforming mindset that helped you pursue the life you want. Be mindful of the choices you are making to create lasting happiness. Be appreciative of how far you have traveled. Stay hopeful for where you are going. Stay focused on who you want to become. Stay expecting good things will unfold in short timeframes. Stay going with the flow that leads to your fruitful future. Stay loving the life you are living. Stay committed to creating all that you desire. Stay positive and believe that everything is working out for you, ahead of you, and with you. Stay believing in your blessings. Life is good.

July 12

I am trusting big, beautiful blessings are on the way to me.

What's unfolding in your life is necessary for clearing the old and ushering in the new. You asked for more, and now you are being prepared and positioned closer to your plenty. Remember, endings are necessary to create beginnings, and change is required for evolution and growth. Make the transformation easier by releasing your resistance. Shift your focus instead toward allowing. Allow yourself to tune in, listen, and be guided to take inspired action. Allow yourself to embrace the support being provided for you. Allow yourself to be Divinely guided to what serves the highest vision for your life. Trust what is coming is more than you can imagine.

July 13

I am moving closer to my victory.

Many people get weary when their dreams feel unattainable. This is the moment most abandon their desires or start over. If you choose to start over, trust you are doing it from a wiser place. If you decide to quit, recall why you started. Before you choose which action to take, check-in with yourself to see if you are just tired with all the trying. When you are fatigued, learn to rest, not quit. When you feel exhausted, find the test that is causing resistance to your progress. You don't always have to start over; you just have to find the missing lesson and master it. Take a break to realign, reset, then move forward with clarity, solutions, and strength. Remember, there will be times to stand still and times to make moves. Awareness of what you need will help you maintain momentum.

July 14

I am mastering my peace.

Sometimes, your life must be broken down and reassessed before it is rebuilt more magnificently than you can imagine. When something isn't constructed correctly, it won't be able to handle future expansion. Destruction is another form of transformation and should not be feared. When you think things are falling apart, trust that you are being rebuilt to embrace the significant blessings coming your way. It might feel challenging to remain positive during these moments of reconstruction, but it is possible. Your happiness will happen when you use all your pieces, even your broken ones, to create your masterpieces. Remember, you are a powerful creator. Every experience is helping you build the highest vision for your life.

July 15

I am receiving clarity and wisdom to overcome.

When you are doubtful, overwhelmed, or stressed, take a moment to pause before you press on. Use this time to pay attention to the limiting beliefs keeping you in a pattern of feeling stuck. Sometimes what you think you cannot achieve will keep you away from what is possible. You can find your way forward by clearing any blockage in your mindset that prevents you from progressing. Always ask for the wisdom to overcome, not for the problem to disappear. Be mindful of the thoughts that affect your happiness. Stop looking back and reliving past limits. Stop looking forward with fear your dreams may not manifest. Start looking for reasons to celebrate the change happening in the present moment.

July 16

I am supportive, and I am supported.

There is a difference between saving, sacrificing, and supporting; you decide which one you give to others. Some people may not want their win the same way you want it for them. It is not your responsibility to save others, but you can support them by inspiring them. Words aren't the best teacher; action is where most people get their motivation. Do what you can, encourage them, offer guidance, but know everyone must save themselves. Stop sacrificing your happiness for others to find theirs. Everyone is responsible for their joy. You are the only one that can show up and support your life vision. The way you live your life will inspire others to step up and create what they desire.

July 17

I am destined for more.

Life never takes anything from you without replacing it with something better. Pay attention to your experiences; they reveal where you should expand your mindset and make room for more blessings. If you are being shown that you should walk away from something or someone, let it go. If you are being redirected after a closed door, change course. If you are being made to wait, continue to be patient and prepare for receiving more. Life is always giving you the Divine guidance you need to head in the direction of your unlimited possibilities. Remember, you asked for more; you are being guided there whether you understand the process or not. You are worthy, you are enough, and you are destined for more.

July 18

I am focused on creating solutions.

Yes, fear can keep you from creating change, but trust you have what it takes to push past anything that impacts your progress. Don't let the fear of what could happen; make it that nothing happens. When you are doubtful, your beliefs are not aligned with the truth of what you can create. Remember, a belief is a thought you continue to think, and it can be changed. Get out of your way and stop giving control to your doubts. Give power instead to your possibilities. If you focus on what can't be done, you cannot empower what you can get done. Push past the inner distress by concentrating on creating solutions. Remember, a problem cannot exist without a solution.

July 19

I am grateful for my progress.

Be grateful for your progress while you work on where you want to go. You believed in the possibility of your dreams even though you weren't fully clear about how you would get there. Where you are right now was once a goal. Give yourself credit for starting. You didn't allow the unknown to keep you from going after your all. Yes, your reality was challenging, but you kept going by trusting. Acknowledge your commitment to your happiness. Be proud of everything you do to make the life you want happen. You have what it takes to create more. Keep working on your mental might and your positive feelings. The Universe is continually working to remove the obstacles you cannot see. Stay the course. You've got this.

July 20

I am leveling up and becoming the best version of myself.

Spiritual growth does not happen when you pray; it occurs as you navigate your challenges and transform your relationship with yourself. It is in the trying times you develop your patience, inner peace, and persistence with faith. It is the journey that allows you to become the person that pursues all that you desire, not the destination. Use your experiences to keep leveling up to where you want to go. Becoming the best version of yourself in every phase will get you to the next stage. When you feel like giving up, remember the path you took to be where you are right now. Keep expanding, creating desires, and attaining more. Life is about learning, living, and enjoying the process.

July 21

I am releasing, healing, and thriving.

You make the shift from surviving to thriving when you accept that your experiences do not define you; they strengthen and shape you. Letting go, healing and forgiveness are necessary aspects of embracing where you want to go. Never let what is behind you prevent you from planting solid roots where you are right now. Keep planning for the future and release what happened in the past. Who you become will flourish when you remember only you can produce your more. Always trust in your ability to create what you want. Use what is created within you to create a new you. Work on how you thrive on the inside, and it will blossom on the outside. Keep focusing on how you want to feel.

July 22

I am worthy, and I am Divinely supported.

Time always reveals what's meant to stay in your life. Sometimes what is clearing is only making room for more. Don't let your doubt about better arriving signal to the Universe that you don't believe in what you deserve. Let what wants to leave fade away with ease. Trust that more significant blessings are coming and get ready for them. Ask yourself what you need to do today to get prepared for your more tomorrow. Remember, what's meant for you is constantly flowing to you. When the clearing is over, you will be amazed at how worthy the Universe already thinks you are. Meet your happiness halfway by trusting the process. Allow the desires you want to unfold right on time.

July 23

I am showing up every day for my success.

Everyone has moments where they lack confidence or feel stuck. Those are the days that define your persistence. Don't let one challenging day deter you from seeing better days. Take time to find the reason you feel defeated. To regain your sureness, acknowledge the change that is already unfolding. Every day you wake, you are on your way to achieving more. Remember, you are constantly expanding, asking, and moving closer to what you want. You have what it takes to bounce back from any moment of uncertainty. Show up on your tough days, best days, and every in-between day. You are always making progress. Celebrate your commitment to your growth.

July 24

I am cultivating better daily habits.

Many people are focused on improving their lives but don't work on who they are or cultivate better daily thoughts and habits. You are the creator of your experiences. Once you understand this, you see that the real work is your relationship with yourself. It is how you think and speak of your capabilities that make a difference. To create your best life, you must develop healthier belief patterns. No one says you have to be perfect; you just have to work at perfecting who you think and believe you are. If you are a good starter, consider yourself the best finisher. If you are an excellent visionary, believe you are the best implementer. You are the one who determines how you design what you desire.

July 25

I am aligning with the fullness of who I am.

Every experience has two opposing sides. For every loss, there is life waiting to be accepted. For every blunder, there is a blessing waiting to blossom. For every period of darkness, there is light waiting to enter. You cannot understand one without experiencing the other. When you expect only triumphs, you don't prepare yourself for the trials. It is sometimes hard to grasp that this is the way, but what you go through shows you where you need to go and who you need to be to get there. Good times are easy, but they are not where you develop the confidence to be fully you. What you don't want is always guiding you to what you do want. Experiences are where you learn to define your preferences.

July 26

I am good enough to receive the best life has to offer.

Many people battle with believing they aren't good enough because they were told they must be perfect to win. This isn't right. To be human is to evolve constantly and to succeed at growth, you must learn flexibility. Perfection is impossible and does not determine value. Stop delaying your progress by putting pressure on yourself to live an unattainable life. Failures allow you to flourish because they give you something to improve. Every 'missed take' can be retried from a new place of wisdom, not regret. Life is all about becoming the best you, not the perfect you. Remember always, you are enough, and you are doing enough. You are deserving. Flow confidently and create all you desire.

July 27

I am getting better, and I am flourishing.

Believe you are always getting better, and in every moment, you are flourishing. You have made mindset improvements that brought you great accomplishments. You have released the past burdens you were never meant to carry. You have created a belief system that enables your ability to overcome. You have kept on rising despite the challenge of the climb. Understand that now is your time and keep showing up and stepping up. Today applaud and celebrate all that you have done to live the life you want. Embrace and empower the new you that you are becoming. Keep trusting everything is always working out in your favor. What is yours will arrive right on time.

July 28

I am strong, and I am committed to my happiness.

No matter what cards you have been dealt today, trust that you will win no matter what you think you hold. Staying in the game and not giving up will bring you the blessings you want to welcome. What you see right now does not determine what you can manifest for your future. Learn to bet on your success because you believe in yourself and your abilities. You are very capable of producing the life you want. Be strong. Stay committed to your happiness. What is yours will always find you. What is coming to you will always show up for you. Do the work to align with it as best you can. Keep trusting the process that produces your plenty. Remember, there is always more.

July 29

I am patient as my dreams materialize.

The Universe knows every single wish you made and is always working to bring it closer to you. You cannot take back what you have asked for; you can only add to it and make your request bigger. What you want will happen. Keep believing and working on being the person that is ready to receive it. The right preparation is key to any successful journey. Remember, blessings have a way of manifesting when you release them to Divine timing. When you let go of how, when, and why, what you want will show up bigger than you thought, faster than you can imagine, and more rewarding than you dreamed possible. Be patient and allow your dreams to mature into more.

July 30

I am changing my focus and taking action.

Sometimes what holds you back is your belief that 'something' is holding you back. Nothing is in your way but your mindset. Not all your thoughts are true, and they may be what's blocking your success. The faster you correct your thinking, the quicker you get out of your way. Start with changing your focus from 'can't' to constructing. You have to believe you can achieve before you can receive. Put all your thoughts into trusting in the unlimited possibilities of your potential. Work on your emotional, physical, and spiritual worthiness. Release what does not serve you to find what strengthens you to move forward. Remember, you are a powerful creator. Create the life you want.

July 31

I am discovering my true magic.

Love yourself enough to give yourself everything you ever wanted. Know that while you do the work, you will continue to have experiences that make you want to create more. Challenges help you develop the skills needed to keep succeeding. Don't try to skip the lessons; conquer them and enable yourself to climb even further. They are where you uncover that you are the magic ingredient. No moment is ever wasted as they all transform you into the person that builds your empire. Keep developing the techniques that enable you to triumph. Be satisfied with all the efforts you are making. Manifestations will keep repeatedly happening when you master a winning mindset. The more you use what you know the more you create what you want.

August 01

I am at peace.

This August, I surrender the need to control my life's timing and allow the Universe to bring abundant goodness to me. I am grateful for what I have accomplished. I am gracefully releasing what doesn't serve me. I am contented with the miracles manifesting. I am focused forward on the highest vision for my life. I am mastering the mindset that allows me to thrive. I am trusting things are always working out for me. I am taking inspired action. I am appreciating what is showing up for me and I am using my experiences to create more. I am living in the moment with a peace of mind. I am delighting in the goodness in my life. I am the point of attraction and everything I want comes easily to me. I am blessed.

August 02

I am using what I have to level up to more.

Many people aren't satisfied with what they have, which discourages them from pursuing what they want. How can you get more if you aren't happy with what you already possess? Yes, you may not have all you desire, but your attention to the lack is the same as focusing on the problem and wondering why you can't find a solution. Take another look at where you are and what you have. The answer to creating more is right there. Use gratitude for where you are to create more of where you want to go. Acknowledge that you are not in the same place you started; you are further along than before. Start where you are to level up to more.

August 03

I am releasing my resistance.

Yes, it is a natural response to see change as challenging, but it is not too late for you to take control of your choices. It's not too late to start something new. It's not too late for you to work on what you want. It's not too late for you to pursue your happiness. It's not too late to release the limiting mindset that holds you back. It is not too late to understand the fullness of what you deserve. Trust the transformation you are experiencing will not happen overnight, but it will lead to lifelong blessings. Do your part to move it along faster by accepting what is happening. This will help you release your resistance. Take it one day at a time. Before you know it, you will be delivered to the other side. Remember, nothing strong is built in a day; that also includes you.

August 04

I am focused on my flourishing.

To thrive is to pursue what makes you prosper. To survive is to give yourself the minimum effort to live. You have the choice with which you give your attention. Don't stay stuck surviving because you are waiting for more to manifest. Thrive by making a daily decision to be grateful and stay positively focused on solutions despite the circumstances. You will flourish in every moment you decide to make your happiness a priority. Only you can move from surviving to thriving. Start with being mindful about how you set out to live your life daily. You alone control how you get up, get out, go after all that you see possible for your life. Be good to yourself, and life will be good to you. Keep appreciating all your efforts.

August 05

I am satisfied with my journey to creating more.

If you believe that "when" life gets better, everything will be better, you are setting yourself up for disappointment. The only way to be happy is to feel satisfied with your journey of creating more. You will always have desires; this will never end. You are the same person with the same emotions, no matter where you are or what you have. You are the constant; the journey is the change. Contentment, while you create, is the key to lasting happiness. You have one journey through this lifetime. Make the most of it by enjoying it. Work on how you want to feel and who you are before the results show up. This will make what you desire manifest faster. Delight in the life you are living.

August 06

I am always supported.

When you think things are working against you, recognize you are only being guided to more than you can imagine for yourself. Most people's journey is one of worthiness in what they can create. Life is constantly showing you how to move from what you don't want by helping you define what you do want. Experiencing disappointment is where you develop your determination to find happiness. Experiencing a lack is where you appreciate the opportunities to pursue more. Experiencing rejection is where you learn to value who you are. Experiencing failure is where you develop the technique it takes to go for the win. Experiences reveal what you need to thrive before your more arrives. Life is amazing because it is always on your side.

August 07

I am a powerful creator on my path to more.

Celebrate that you made it through a challenge. Highlighting your positives will help you feel empowered to keep going. Remember, the person that goes into the storm is never the same soul that steps out. They are stronger and wiser. Appreciating your experiences will help you enjoy your sunlight. Keep staying positive on the journey that makes you a powerful creator on your path. Leave all storms behind you. They were meant to nourish you and not be carried by you. You owe it to yourself to go after everything you prayed for in the rain. When the clouds clear, the sun will shine and bless the next version of you. Take a moment to bask in the light of your leveling up.

August 08

I am already blessed.

It is impossible to learn how to manifest everything you need to live the life you desire all at once. This is why life develops your creative abilities throughout your journey. Experiences teach you how to want more. You cannot get everything you desire in one request, but you can create everything you want through your persistence. Remember, happiness is not when everything falls into place; it is your ability to recognize the Divine miracle of blessings falling into place. Have patience; what you want is always coming because you are always creating. What is for you always shows up when you are ready. Trust you are being positioned for your plenty. Be amazed by the miracle, not the momentum. You are already blessed.

August 09

I am reconnecting to my confidence and redirecting my life.

Today give yourself patience, love, compassion, and find your peace. Give yourself credit for the patience it takes to wait for more. Give yourself love and remember that you are enough. Give yourself compassion and commit to working on your happiness. Give yourself peace and release the pace of your progress. You are doing the best you know with what you have learned. Keep creating and believing in your dreams. You are limitless possibilities, and you deserve what's best for you and your happiness. Today reconnect with you and give yourself the confidence you need to redirect your life anywhere you desire.

August 10

I am focused on winning.

Life can occasionally feel overwhelming, but remember, you are very capable of overcoming anything on your path. Blocks are designed to strengthen you for more blessings. Significant dreams are not created in comfort zones. You will always be sent a challenge that reveals the mighty warrior within you. Triumph, and don't get distracted by the battle. Focus instead on your victory. When you concentrate on the promise, you understand the fight always has a purpose. Most people work on what they want, but successful people work on who they need to become to live the life they desire. Trust in every moment; you are gaining momentum towards the highest vision for your life. Find what makes you emotionally thrive, and it will inspire you to flourish in all areas.

August 11

I am taking the time to discover my greatness.

What has materialized on the outside should never distract you from working on who you are on the inside. Happiness is an inside job that manifests throughout your life when you actively work on feeling good daily. If you don't find contentment with what you have and where you are, it is difficult to feel satisfied with your life. Therefore, who you are on the inside is very important to your overall well-being and ability to create more. Feeling abundant, peaceful, safe, confident, loved, or successful starts with you. Remember, they are all emotions you create. Make the time today to go within and discover your greatness by intentionally focusing on how you want to feel and who you are.

August 12

I am unlocking my full potential.

Remember, every up, down, yes, and no has taught you something; focus on the similarities. They are the secret to your fulfillment. Start with daydreaming about what you want from today forward. If you had no limits, what would you do with your life? Finding your purpose begins with spending time to discover what your soul desires. Once you figure out how you want to live, look at the skills you possess. Most people overlook their most significant asset because it is the most natural thing for them to create. It could be as simple as the way you think. It will feel like love, not labor. Everything you need to succeed is already within you. You have what it takes to create the life you most desire. Find what feels good and do more of it. It will lead to a life well lived.

August 13

I am saying yes to peace and prosperity.

Today get hopeful and expect that everything is always working out for you. You have to expect good things before you receive good things. Today say yes to the peace and prosperity that is becoming a natural way of life for you. Say yes to the love that's available and abundant around you. Say yes to the purpose that is being revealed to you. Say yes to the support and the growing opportunities that show up for you. Say yes to the healing and wholeness growing within you. Say yes to the doors opening up for you. Say yes to paths clearing ahead of you. Say yes to the manifestations gaining momentum for you. Mostly and triumphantly, say yes to all the blessings making their way toward you.

August 14

I am growing my all.

Everyone prays for big blessings to manifest but fail to recognize the power of small starts. You have to begin your journey somewhere. Baby steps are still considered steps because they are moving you forward. Do not disregard a movement that begins as small; trust it will build momentum. Don't focus on the length of your stride; focus on its quality and consistency. A short yet confident step forward can bridge the gap to your happiness. The talents or abilities you see as unimportant have the potential to bring you significant abundance. Those hard times you overcame, those lessons you learned, strengthened your abilities within to win. With time and nurturing, your small will grow into your ALL.

August 15

I am stepping out, showing up, and shining at my brightest.

Don't doubt your talents; they were never given to be hidden. Have faith in your ability to create opportunities to thrive. Don't wait to be discovered. Focus on sharing who you are, not perfecting what you are doing. The more you share, the more comfortable you will be at shining. How else will you be seen if you don't present yourself? Start and give your gifts time and patience to blossom into more. Keep using what you love to create the life vision you desire. Make room for miracles, step out, show up, and shine. The Universe wants to bless you with unlimited possibilities to prosper. Meet life where it is trying to meet you, at the intersection of using your talent and thriving.

August 16

I am allowing myself to rest and reset before I step forward.

Just beyond moments of weariness are the wins. Everyone occasionally gets exhausted and wants to give up. Right before the manifestation of your dreams, you will know it. This is when fear creeps in and convinces you that you are at the point of failure and should stop. There is a difference between giving up and taking a rest. Don't let doubt keep you from continuing your journey. You made progress despite not knowing if your efforts would work. Acknowledge your courage to start. Today, reset and find what will empower you to step forward. Refuel your mind, body, and spirit before you advance. Sometimes you must go through neutral before you push it into drive.

August 17

I am ALL ways being blessed.

Consider your obstacles detours to your blessings. They may appear as blocks, but they are Divinely sent to redirect you to the easiest path to your happiness. Before you become discouraged with the process, remember you asked for more, and you are only being guided there. Today, don't dwell on what isn't going your way; focus on improving your emotional well-being. Instead of feeling stuck, choose to spend your energy improving your mindset about where you are. Only you can create more through the choices you make. You have the ability and the knowledge to transform blocks into abundant blessings. Trust in your abilities. Delays can help you practice patience while preparing for your prosperity. Remember, what's yours is yours and cannot be denied.

August 18

I am grateful, and I am being blessed with more.

Keep trusting and asking for the ability to overcome anything that does not serve your happiness. In experiencing absence, you learned appreciation. In being down, you understood up. In knowing struggle, you recognized success. In giving, you began to appreciate receiving. Not having what you want isn't an indication you have failed; it is a clear direction to what you desire. Don't let anything stop you from going after your all. Confidently embrace any 'no' and step forward to your 'yes.' Remember, life is continually working to remove the obstacles you cannot see. Be grateful for your blessings while you work on more. What is yours can never be denied, delayed, or diverted.

August 19

I am always given what I need to thrive.

Say goodbye to whatever wants to go; release it with grace. Say hello to the blessings coming; welcome them with gratitude. Focus on what is present; trust more will come. When you think you were neglected, the Universe will show you it was silently preparing more than you can imagine. Don't lose hope because you cannot see a way, rejoice and expect your miracle. You are always given what you need to thrive. Anything you wish to build, you have to be built for it. Allow your lessons to level you up to where you want to go. Trust everything is always working out for you. You are on the right path. If you can dream it, you can develop it into your reality. More will manifest soon.

August 20

I am showing up for my happiness.

No matter what you have overcome, or how far you have travelled, trust that you are always doing the best you can. The moon is the most remarkable example that you don't have to be whole every day to shine. It's the days you decide to show up despite your doubt, that define and develop your persistence. Don't let one day where you don't feel your best deter you from seeing your better days. There is a purpose to all things at all times. You have what it takes to make every moment count. Show up on your tough days, best days, and every in-between day. Just a little extra effort daily is all you need to make your life extraordinary. All efforts count. Keep creating and building your confidence.

August 21

I am a winner, and I know it.

Everyone wants to succeed because they believe it will make them happy. However, most become impatient with the process because they need to see their win before they are satisfied. When you feel good before what you want materializes, you will be amazed at how fast the Universe will serve it up. Happiness is not always about the manifestation; it is about the manifesting and enjoying the process of things falling into place. Marvel at how well you are Divinely supported, protected and provided for at all times. That is where the beauty and joy in life reside. Acknowledging how well things are always working out for you will make you expectant of even more. Try feeling successful now and see how easily the victory flows to you. Feel like a winner before you welcome your win.

August 22

I am celebrating my commitment to my happiness.

You are getting better; you are flourishing. You are making improvements with your mindset and releasing your limits. You have celebrated your progress by acknowledging your commitment to your happiness. You have created a belief in your ability to overcome, and you keep climbing. You recognize that now is your time and you are showing up and stepping up. Today take a moment to bask in the sunshine of all you have done. You are doing a great job with your life. Be proud of who you are and embrace who you are becoming. You are good to yourself, expect life to be just as good as you keep creating. You are worthy of unlimited abundance. You are blessed.

August 23

I am welcoming big wins.

When you concentrate on your promise, you understand that every challenge has a purpose. At this moment, decide if you are a worrier or a warrior. The art of war says to concentrate on the plan for victory and not get distracted by the battle's difficulty. Remember, fights are necessary to reveal the warrior within and strengthen your skills to win. Develop your technique to thrive, and you will overcome. Choose creative strategy over emotional struggle and welcome your victory. Most people work on where they want to go and never master who they are. Work on who you are being, and it will improve how you are doing. The more skilled you are at living life, the more successful you will become. You have what it takes to have it all.

August 24

I am faithful that things are working out in my favor.

Setups get you where you want to go, and setbacks redirect you to where you need to be. What you want and need are two different things. Shifting between both is part of the natural cycle of life. Learning to embrace constant change is the lesson that takes most people the longest to learn. You have asked for more, don't try to control how it should happen. Have faith in the process because every up, down, back, and forth has a purpose. Get out of your way, allow forces more significant than you to get you more of what you want faster. Believe things are working out for you. Faith and gratitude will give you the courage to keep going despite what you cannot see. Your work is to prepare to receive. You've got this.

August 25

I am working on my win.

Do not choose misery over miracles because you are not willing to put in the work on your well-being. Many are stuck in places they do not desire because they refuse to push themselves to better. You have to want what you have asked for and be willing to do the work needed. Spiritual growth does not happen when you pray; it occurs when you are transformed through your challenges. Emotional growth does not happen when you are happy; it happens when you push past your tears and choose to work at your well-being. Your miracle is only one action away. You know what you need to do to thrive. Focus on how you want to feel and live. Don't let struggle keep you from making that critical step toward your success. Don't wish for better; work on creating the best.

August 26

I am worthy, and I am priceless.

When you begin to understand what you are worth, your life transforms beyond your wildest dreams. The belief that you are deserving of ALL allows you to reach for more, welcome more, and go after more. You begin to see that you were never broken; you were only being pushed to blossom beyond what you believed was possible for yourself. You remember that you were always whole, and you only needed a reason to flourish. You accept that lack was only a lesson, and you are capable of building your abundance. Only you can define how valuable you are, then set the expectation for others. You are the point of attraction; invite your success. You already know your true worth; remember it. You are priceless. Start practicing what that means to you daily.

August 27

I am destined for big, beautiful blessings.

Life will occasionally present a challenge to help you grow. Trust it is only encouraging you to step out of your comfort zones and closer to your desires. It is okay to want to stay safe, but sometimes you are invited to use your fear to push you toward flourishing. Don't refuse the invitation to better, level up to your bigger. You asked for abundance, love, and success; you are being taken there. Step up, step out, and never look back. Sometimes the thing you are holding on to is limiting your growth. Your dreams may be more significant than where you are willing to stay. Get excited that you are being set on a path of prosperity. Where you are is too small for who you are.

August 28

I am celebrating that I am still standing and going.

Mistakes do not mean you are disqualified; consider it time out to readjust your technique before you reenter the race. The beautiful thing about life is that it gives you unlimited chances to pursue success after setbacks. Don't beat yourself up because you stumbled; celebrate that you are still standing. Remember, you are never failing at anything; you are always learning how to master everything. Use the lesson to sharpen your skills before you step forward. Trust that you are only being prepared for where you are going. Enjoy the process that gets you all that you have dreamed of having. Every day, choose to start stronger from where you are standing. Keep going, my friend!

August 29

I am mastering my moves to more.

Consider patience a lesson designed to strengthen you in the art of receiving. Time reveals the significance of what you truly deserve. If you are not fully prepared, getting all of your blessings at once can be overwhelming. The waiting is teaching you the skills needed to manage it all. No one is born knowing everything; they learn what they need along the way. This is the same for blessings; they will show up when you are ready for them. It's in the meantime you master the next time. The bigger the desires, the more momentum is required to create its fullness. The journey is where the joy is; the destination is where it all ends. Stop rushing life. Start relishing it. Trust the timing of your life.

August 30

I am empowering myself to move forward.

Every phase of life teaches you how to direct your attention toward what you need to thrive through each experience. Each stage is designed to strengthen an aspect of who you are and further prepare you for where you are going. Life is always showing you how to bless all that blesses you. Stay persistent about pouring into what fills you and what feels good. You can always find peace through what makes you happy. If you are always rushing to get to the end, you miss the joy experienced in the middle. Focus on what you need to empower your happiness, and you will always keep moving forward. Sometimes the lesson is about gratitude for all your experiences.

August 31

I am tuning in for guidance.

Pleasant feelings can be easy, but the uncomfortable ones are challenging. They are only pushing you to listen to what you need. Pay attention; your soul is trying to communicate with you. When you aren't feeling your best, you may be disconnected from who you are. When you focused on what is not happening, you miss what is unfolding. You have asked for happiness, love, peace, and abundance; life is always trying to guide you there. The Source within you knows that you are always loved, safe, supported, protected, and creating more. If you are currently fighting to hold onto the old, let it go. Imagine the strength you will have to create something new. Listen in to your soul for how. It is always available to support your every move. Allow it to guide you to your more.

September 01

I am supported on my journey to creating more.

This September, I am ready for all new blessings. My new connections will inspire me to be the best version of myself. My new opportunities will materialize and lead me to my abundance. My new clarity will help me focus on setting the right intentions for my future. My new mindset will support my success on my journey. New doors will open to better paths and better prospects. New improvements will allow me to succeed in my pursuit of what I desire. New ways to find what makes my heart happy and my soul inspired. New moments of joy, fulfillment, and solutions will lead to creating the life I deserve. Most of all, I welcome new miracles manifesting daily.

September 02

I am aware of my full worth.

Are you focused on being seen when you meet others, or are you concentrated on sharing who you genuinely are? Many people don't recognize there is a difference between the two. When your goal is to be seen, you distract yourself from being who you are. This shifts your focus toward what others are willing to give, not what they are offering. Don't set yourself up for the constant need for the validation of others. Focus instead on being true by sharing yourself. Your authenticity will produce your well-being and improve the type of people that surround you. Always share the best of who you are and welcome it to be reciprocated. The more you live your truth, the more you recognize it in others.

September 03

I am Be-coming the best version of myself.

If you spend a lot of time worrying about the future, releasing the control of how you think things should go will bring you some relief. Instead, acknowledge that you aren't supposed to figure it all out at once. Yes, sometimes it's challenging to keep trusting the process, but it is possible. Have faith what you need will arrive right on time. Remember, your power is in your response. Start with working on your ability to BE. BE-ing is about learning who you are. Everyday focus on what you need, and you will gain clarity on how to move forward. It is in BE-ing you BE-come your best version. Focus on your relationship with yourself instead of the results. You are the creator of those results; get to know yourself better.

September 04

I am choosing happiness.

When you woke up today, did you intentionally choose to thrive or survive? To thrive is to prosper purposely. To survive is to just exist without exercising your right to create. To move from surviving to thriving begins with understanding you have a choice every single day. You determine where your attention goes and what you produce. Thriving is the mindful decision to be optimistic despite your circumstances. It is about being focused on solutions rather than the problem. Remember, there is always a way out. Don't stay stuck surviving because you are constantly deferring your happiness to when things get better. Choose to be happy now. Make the decision every day to find contentment for where you are. The inspiration to go further will always arrive.

September 05

I am surrendering the fight and welcoming the win.

Today surrender. Surrender your need to know how and when because you are Divinely supported. Surrender your worry because you are worthy of what you work for. Surrender your lack because focusing on it blocks your abundance. Surrender your stress because it is easier to go with the flow. Surrender to the pace because you are always making progress. Surrender your constant need to act; remember you are the point of attraction, allow things to come to you. Surrender your overthinking and make mental room to receive the solution. Surrender your heart to healing and welcome the wholeness. Surrender the fight because everything is ALL WAYS working out for you.

September 06

I am blessed with what I need.

Do not limit your life vision to your current circumstances. This moment in time is small compared to the bigness of who you can become. If you believe that "when" life gets better, you will feel better, you will remain emotionally stuck where you are. If you keep looking for joy in people, places, and things, it will show up but provide temporary satisfaction and relief. The only way to feel lifelong happiness is to create the feeling in every moment. When you work on how you want to feel, the results will show up in all areas of your life. Things don't have to change for you to live better; you just have to feel better for things to change. Remember, you already have what you need to succeed. Start thriving by focusing on your emotional well-being.

September 07

I am moving in the direction I am destined to go.

You are always moving forward. When you recognize that even blocks are working in your favor, you release your worry. Be thankful for every closed door, blocked path, or 'no' you have encountered; it helped you develop your decision to go for more. What you don't want is always leading you to the path that delivers what you do want. Sometimes when you ask for better, the Universe will respond by redirecting and rearranging your entire life before presenting the resolution and the restoration. Resisting the change will make the transition challenging. Release your limits with ease. Remember, what was blocking your blessings must be cleared to create your possibilities. Trust the process.

September 08

I am prioritizing what makes me feel good.

You cannot live a happy life when you repeatedly put your well-being at the bottom of your to-do list. Practice putting yourself first every single day. The better you are, the best you can be for others. No one can effectively build a life of prosperity with their happiness behind everything else. You cannot expect blessings for things you aren't committed to creating. Self-first is not selfish when it is focused on the proper habits that support your emotional, spiritual, and physical thriving. Being your best self should be your primary focus in all things you do. When you feel good, you build a beautiful life and stronger connections with others. You thrive when you prioritize your well-being.

September 9

I am trusting then doing.

Your life is unfolding as it should. Every phase is important to the next. You are always preparing who you are for where you are going. What you need at every stage will be provided when you get there. Don't focus on figuring out future steps; instead, give attention to enjoying what you are doing and where you are right now. Don't try to understand how it will all come together; just believe you are being guided and supported on your journey. At this moment you have everything you need. If for any reason you doubt your potential, remember, you can't manifest what you don't think is possible. Trust it is yours first, then it will show up. Make your daily work about improving your well-being. You create tomorrow by what you believe you deserve today.

September 10

I am believing in all my possibilities.

Whatever you asked for, work on understanding what it feels like to have it before it fully manifests in the form you desire. When you want love, start with accepting who you are. When you want support, believe in your potential. When you want peace, align with what your soul says it needs. When you want to build your faith, push past your fears to what feels right. When you want to move forward, forgive yesterday. When you want abundance, see how blessed you already are. Consistently take inventory of what is available to you in the now. The more you appreciate what you have, the more blessings will show up. Everything you desire starts with you. Practice the possibility of its reality daily.

September 11

I am expecting my miracles to manifest soon.

Delays are not denials; they are blessings that allow you to work on creating more. While you wait on the manifestation, use the opportunity to clarify, add more specifics, and fine-tune your desires. Setbacks help you better define what happiness means to you. Remember, there must be a problem to solve before you have the pleasure of solutions. Life is about sifting and sorting through what you need to thrive. Marvel at how things miraculously fall into place and celebrate how great you are at creating. The unfolding is where the biggest miracles happen. Enjoy the spontaneous surprises that show up along the way. You are never waiting; you are constantly building and asking for more.

September 12

I am aligning with my true self.

When your energy feels off-centered, you aren't aligned with your true self. Imbalance is an indication that you need to pay attention to your thoughts and emotions. Remember, a belief is a thought you continue to think, and a feeling is an emotional state of being. Your emotions can be influenced by what you are thinking. The heart and the head experience conflict when one believes differently from what the other feels. Your peace will come from your constant awareness of how negative thoughts can produce your undesirable feelings. To realign yourself, take a second to tune into both and sort out the facts. Know the difference between created and true feelings or beliefs. The more you practice mindfulness, the better you become at aligning with your truth.

September 13

I am confidently moving forward to better.

Don't lose hope when challenging patterns emerge. Instead, focus on developing the skills you need to create solutions. Life will keep sending the same lesson until you learn to release the self-imposed limits that keep you from realizing your full potential. Let go of the beliefs you have created around worthiness and work on improving your mindset. Remember, you are worthy of having all that you can imagine. You are enough as you are. You are very capable of pursuing your dreams. You are deserving of everything you desire. Whatever experience you keep repeating, compassionately face it, courageously find the lesson, then fix it. Confidently move forward to your better.

September 14

I am beautiful, strong, remarkable, and loving.

When you find yourself going above and beyond because you fear losing affection, take a step back and honestly look at the value you bring. Stop taking less because you keep forgetting your full worth. Know that you don't need the acceptance of others, only to believe in yourself and your full potential. Release the need for external validation of your extraordinary abilities. Be proud of who you are and what you have achieved. You are beautiful, strong, capable, supported, provided for, remarkable, and loving. You have successfully gotten yourself this far along your journey and will continue to take yourself to unimaginable places. Believe in what you are capable of creating.

September 15

I am building my momentum to more with gratitude.

You are exactly where you need to be right now. You cannot go back and fix where you have been, but you can choose to focus on moving forward. Decide at this moment where your attention goes. Will your time be spent looking at what you have not achieved, or will it be filled with gratitude and celebration of how much you have accomplished? Stay present, and you will see you are already being blessed beyond measure. The components of your dreams are all falling into place right on time. Appreciation for your progress builds momentum for lasting fulfillment. Enthusiasm for life happens in the moments you stay present and count your blessings.

September 16

I am receiving all good things.

You are working very hard to win; place the same effort into your healing. Healing is about releasing the past's influence on your present. When you bring what happened into what is happening, you allow your history to take over your now. Healing will help you master the mindset you need to manifest everything you are working on for your future. Remember, every experience is designed to advance you, not keep you trapped in a cycle. You have what it takes to create from the present, not from the past. Make your emotional, mental, physical, and spiritual well-being your primary focus, and you will find what you need to keep thriving. Be grateful for where you are and get excited about where you are going. Trust everything you need to succeed will be provided for you right on time.

September 17

I am expecting my miracles to manifest soon.

Today, create the change you desire by concentrating on something different. If you are struggling, keep fighting and have faith you will move forward. If you have been sacrificing, don't give up; know you will succeed. If you feel defeated, remember help is always available and you will attract the support you need. If you are doubting, direct your attention towards doing what needs to get done. Remember, just as every coin has two sides, problems always have solutions; it is a universal law. Wherever you are, believe that life will always get better. Keep going, keep showing up, and refuse to leave before your miracle happens. You are always manifesting more.

September 18

I am elevating to more good things.

Be thankful you are obstructed from what you thought you wanted. Believe you are being blessed with what you never knew you needed. Whatever you feel is blocking you is Divinely sent to create the ultimate you. Sometimes where you are can limit the view of your possibilities. You are destined for a life vision more significant than you can perceive. Life is always working for you, ahead of you, and with you to produce your desires. It will push you to elevate beyond comfort zones and pull you to levels that help you release your limits. Before you level up, you will be shown how to remove all that holds you back. Stay grateful, and remember you are becoming better for it all.

September 19

I am efficiently creating my more.

When difficult times appear, it is okay to become discouraged. However, don't let one challenge keep you from creating more. Trust you are doing the best you can with what you know. "Everything is working out for me," tell yourself that as many times a day as you need to regain confidence in where you are. Trust in it all; you are not where you are by chance. Remember, every twist, turn, up, and down is necessary for the plan to fall into place. An exciting life is not created from straight lines. The joy on the journey comes from the surprises that show up after the twists and turns. The faster you learn to see the purpose of ALL, the more efficiently you create your MORE.

September 20

I am showing up every single day I am given.

Not every day will be a great day, and that's okay, but trust every day is a beneficial day. On some days, you will be tired of the fight, don't give up; keep going. Use those challenging days to help you define more of what you want. On other days you will feel unproductive. Use those recharge days to rest and recoup. You can always choose to continue building tomorrow. Appreciate all the time given, no matter where you are on the journey. Your effort to build the life you want is never wasted. Continue to be grateful for the abundance of goodness in the simple things. Remember to celebrate your progress every single day. Show up on all the days and just do your best.

September 21

I am creating the change I desire.

Trusting and allowing things to unfold naturally is a great skill to master. The need to control how and when things should happen only challenges your faith in your ability to create what you desire. You don't always end up where you thought you would be, but you always end up where you need to be. Just because you did not arrive in your timeframe does not mean your dreams were denied. Believe in yourself more. You are already doing a great job at manifesting the life you desire. Remember, your job is to ask, align emotionally, and receive. Despite occasional challenges, keep expecting improvements. Sometimes you are delayed for more significant blessings to be prepared. Everyone has their time in the sun. Your efforts will always pay off.

September 22

I am never giving up on my happiness.

Thank everything and everyone that is no longer a part of your life. What left you was never meant to stay. What remained with you will help you create better. You are never defined by what you have lost; you are always blessed with what you use to build the life you desire. Use the knowledge you have gained to grow all your dreams. Practice gratitude for what you are capable of creating. Enjoy your journey by expressing appreciation for all that shows up. Acknowledge that you have a lot to be thankful for at all times. Claim your success, love, and prosperity daily. Remember, you are deserving of all your wins. Don't forget to thank yourself for not giving up on your happiness.

September 23

I am celebrating my work on my happiness.

Today remember that no matter how many mistakes you have made or how slow your progress might feel, you are still ahead of where you started. Don't let the delay put you in despair. Make today your day by celebrating all that you have done to be where you are. Whatever happens, don’t allow anyone or anything to stop you from fully living and enjoying every moment. Congratulate yourself for getting up and showing up. You will achieve your goals plus more. Open yourself to a new attitude of gratitude, prosperity, and joy. Trust that all is well and move forward with a renewed sense of assurance and hope. Keep going. You are a powerful creator, and all your work will pay off.

September 24

I am expecting great things in my life.

Today, before you get on with your day, take inventory of how blessed you are. You will always have more to celebrate than you acknowledge. No matter how your day unfolds or what you have or haven't achieved, be grateful for the opportunity to try again. Start every morning with positive expectations and end every night with gratitude for experiences earned. Use today's experiences to make tomorrow's expectations your reality. You are never losing; you are constantly learning and being given what you need to succeed. Be grateful for waking up and the new opportunity to go after your all. Focus on your manifested abundance and give thanks for the blessings you know will happen soon.

September 25

I am welcoming my harvest.

Everyone has a specific journey; some are more challenging and more rewarding than others. Make your path easier, give your energy to the right things. Don't focus on what's going wrong; stay focused on what's going right. Today set an intention to create more of what's important to you. Believe you have what you need. Everything is always working out for you. Despite what you see happening, trust all storms end. No matter how overcast it looks right now, believe in the beautiful blue skies just beyond the clouds. Whatever you may be experiencing, focus on the promise, not the planting. Stop fighting the rain; use the rain. Remember, rain cleanses as well as nourishes. Thank every drop as you welcome your harvest. Gardens thrive because of the gardener's positive attention.

September 26

I am committed to my healing and wholeness.

Are you paying attention to what increases your energy and what takes away from it? Your internal guidance system constantly lets you know what you should move away from and where you should go. Make the time daily to listen. Commit yourself to the happiness, healing, and wholeness you want. Yes, you were pushed down, but it is up to you to get back up and push forward. Others can help you up, but it is your responsibility to keep standing and going. Don't stay stuck because you think life is unfair, level up by taking control of your choices. You have what it takes to create the experiences you desire, don't let a few shakeups stop your step up to the top.

September 27

I am making the emotional, mental, and spiritual space for my blessings to arrive.

You cannot keep asking for a big harvest yet refuse to plant anything. Yes, the Universe has the power to manifest what you ask for, but you must create the space emotionally, mentally, and spiritually for it to thrive. Decide what you want your life to look like and put effort into becoming that. The things that feed your soul are the key to your happiness. You thrive when you find what feels good. Focusing on good emotions can help you create a great life. Your forest cannot grow and expand if you don't clear the debris from the land. Make room for your blessings. Manifestation requires work on who you are.

September 28

I am picking sooner.

Sooner or later, you have to change the mindset that holds you back from believing you deserve more. Sooner or later, you have to release resentment and replace it with resilience. Sooner or later, you have to outgrow the limits that keep you small so you can go for bigger. Sooner or later, you have to stop wishing and start working on your dreams. Sooner or later, you have to purge the past and start building your future. You are the one that decides if you pick sooner. The sooner you resolve and evolve through challenges, the faster you can begin to create a new reality. Your clarity about what to do will come from finding the purpose for your current position. Remember, everything is unfolding just as it should. Only you can create your change.

September 29

I am creating a new story.

Tough times don't last, but they do create resilient people. Don't allow an old chapter to keep blocking the blessing of a new story. You have the skills and the Divine support to change what is being created. Start with facing and fixing what holds you back today so that your tomorrow will not be the same as yesterday. When you feel discouraged, remind yourself about the marathons you ran, the mountains you climbed, and the stormy seas you navigated through. Don't let one chapter of defeat rewrite the ending of your book. You have what it takes to win. Remember who you are and keep crushing it. If history has taught you anything, you have always successfully found a way through. Only you can make the next chapter better than the last.

September 30

I am embracing all of who I am.

Miracles are happening in your life every day; appreciate them by acknowledging them. Gratitude allows you to slow down enough to embrace blessings and quicken the pace at which more can manifest. Life is about learning to smell the roses in the garden you are passing through. Even roses have thorns that never take away from their beauty. Embrace all of you to understand more of you. You cannot love who you are and dislike the past that shaped you. Your today was created from what you overcame yesterday. Your strength was developed from pushing against your circumstances while pulling yourself forward. Challenges are never easy and will always stay with you. Remember, the lesson is only your memory; it is not your intelligence. Use what you know to create what you want.

October 01

I am expecting miracles to manifest daily.

This October, I am grateful for the opportunities, blessings, and opened doors that are already arranged for me. I am thankful for the wholeness, grace, generosity, and everlasting favor showing up all around me. I am thankful for the ability to stay patient and keep preparing for my prosperity. I am thankful for my progress and continued commitment to creating my victory. I am thankful for always having what I need to thrive and create the life I desire. I am thankful for always being supported and strengthened through every step I take. I am thankful for all the abundant blessings on the way to me. Today I declare my deep gratitude for all the good things in my life.

October 02

I am trusting that there is always more available to me.

Failure feels final when you don't believe you will be given more chances to win. Broken hearts feel devastating when you don't believe you will ever find love again. Change feels crippling when you believe you are losing out on your dreams. Hitting rock bottom is hard on your confidence when you believe you won't reach the top ever again. Every experience is creating your preferences for more. Remember, as long as you are alive, you can make more requests. Trust everything you ask for will always be given. The next time you find yourself feeling like you have no choices, repeat these words for encouragement, "There is always more." Life never takes anything that it doesn't replace with better.

October 03

I am being guided to my higher purpose.

Remember, twists and turns are temporary and necessary to guide you to the top. Build a faith so strong that you become confident enough not to be doubtful, optimistic enough not to be fearful, and determined enough not to be defeated. Know that what is for you will find you. Your destiny to fulfill a higher purpose will never be denied. Never let a setback keep you from your manifestations. Using your why as your inspiration will keep you going when no one supports your journey to a higher purpose. Before you move forward, give yourself credit for the time you spent going after your happiness. Sometimes it is not what you do; it is why you do it. Your intention behind your dreams, hopes, and desires is everything.

October 04

I am focusing on my happiness daily.

Do you know who you are and what makes you happy? Many people want happiness but aren't even clear what that looks like for them. Use this question to reconnect with yourself, create your choices, and direct your life any way you want. Uncertainty is like standing still; finding what makes you happy will provide a path. If you don't gain clarity about your choices, you prevent yourself from creating anything. All you need to begin is to determine what feels good to you. This will lead to the creation of more. How your happiness is produced and maintained happens with time. Be intentional and patient as you work with your good feelings.

October 05

I am ready for my miracles to manifest soon.

Let the word wait work in your favor. Use it to master your faith as you keep moving forward. Don't allow the delay to cause your doubt. Instead, use the time to develop the skills to win. Never let your circumstances discourage your progress. Keep working on who you need to be to live the life you want. Remember, you are never down to nothing because Source is always up to something. You pushed through, and you still keep giving life your best. Celebrate what you have accomplished. A way is constantly being made for you. Your effort is enough. You are doing enough. You are enough. Trust things are lining up for you, and all you need to do is align with it all.

October 06

I am celebrating my ability to create the life I desire.

Life will strip away anything that distracts you from pursuing your desires. Trust the Universe is only trying to lighten the load you aren't meant to carry into the next chapter. Everything you lose is not a loss; it is a lesson in releasing before you level up. Evidence of your transformation can appear big or small; either way, recognize your life is improving for the better. Today step back and marvel at the miracle of change unfolding in your life. Remember, you are always moving forward. If you don't stop to smell the roses, you won't appreciate the garden of abundance growing around you. Today celebrate all that you are creating. Life is good when you acknowledge the possibilities appearing on your path.

October 07

I am trusting that I belong in a place of blessings.

Decide what you want, then go for it. Everything starts with remembering you can create all that you desire. There is nothing that says you cannot have what you can imagine. Life sends you what you welcome and confidently believe in. Expect all the love, abundance, peace, and joy you pray for to arrive right on time. Ask Source to clear paths, improve conditions, change mindsets, remove limits, provide support, and open more doors. Believing you belong in a place of big blessings is only the beginning of the journey. What is for you will always show up. Remember, you will never have to fight to keep what is meant to stay with you.

October 08

I am creating the best life has to offer.

What will you create today? Will it be happiness, abundance, healing, joy, love, or peace? You are a powerful creator; remember that always. Use what you have been given to build the life you want. Trust you already have what you need to achieve it. All life wants you to do is start; it will get the details done. Be confident; you are capable of doing the work to get the results. Finding your worth is where you will discover your real magic. Trust everything you need for the completion will be provided right on time. Your job is to commit; the Universe will help you complete. Go out there and create the most out of the life you want, and don't apologize for it. It is your life, not anyone else's. You've got this.

October 09

I am releasing my limits.

Experiences are where you release limitations. Challenges are where you strengthen your skills. Finding purpose is where you master your talents. Pushing forward is where you develop the determination to fulfill your destiny. Embrace every part of the process that empowers you to thrive. It is all showing you how to become the essence of what you want to create. When you have a desire, align with the spirit of it first. If you want love, embody it. If you want peace, exude calmness. If you want to be valued, respect your time. If you want to be of worth, remember who you truly are. Don't forget to practice celebrating while you are creating. There is no limit to who you can become because it determines what you can build.

October 10

I am a magnet for real love.

It is not your responsibility to save anyone by loving them into their healing. It is your duty to be your best then share yourself with others. It is everyone's personal choice to restore the wholeness of their own heart. Self-improvement begins with self-love and self-awareness. Who you are on the inside is important to what you can create on the outside. Remember, you are the point of attraction. What you want comes to you when you have internally prepared for it. A healed heart recognizes another healed heart and knows real love when it arrives. Focus on who you need to become to attract the life you want to welcome. Most importantly, don't judge yourself while you try. Every choice you make will help you create more of what you want.

October 11

I am making great choices.

Try not to make decisions when you don't feel self-confident about where you are or where you want to go. Choices made from feelings like fear, lack, or loneliness may leave you unhappy. Step back and find what your soul needs to move forward. First, get clear about the why then the how will unfold. Step away from the chaos and get still. Only a quiet heart can find peace, and a focused mind can hear Divine guidance. Abundance flows when you understand your worth. Love grows when you appreciate who you are. Support shows up when you believe in who you are destined to be. Clarity is life's best compass. The more you tune in, the easier it is to recognize what clouds your ability to create the life you want. Get to know who you are, and you will hear where to go.

October 12

I am grateful for my blessings and my chances.

Continue to work on your healing by finding what fills your heart and balances your soul. Pursuing happiness after disappointment requires bravery, commitment, and action. Responses made with self-compassion make moving past mistakes more manageable. Believe that life will get better by developing the discipline to act and go after the best. You can create better from one choice at a time. Remember, mistakes are only missed steps that can be retaken. Regroup, refocus, realign your efforts, and always keep stepping forward. Don't get stuck on a missed step; keep thanking and trusting in your possibilities. When you practice gratitude, the Universe will give you more to appreciate.

October 13

I am triumphing through it all.

Faith does not free you from having to fight for what you want. Dedication to others does not deflect potential disappointment. Hard work does not mean you will never face scarcity or struggle. Being kind does not guarantee you good things will always happen. Experiences are necessary for your evolution; it is where you create preferences and grow. When life isn't going according to plan, choose to operate from a place of wholeness, and your values will shift. You will develop the confidence to go for what you want, and nothing gets in your way. You will release the thoughts and habits that hold you back from pursuing more. You will commit to the actions that create your happiness. You will begin to understand what you deserve and who you truly are. You will create your best life.

October 14

I am welcoming what empowers me to thrive.

Remember, you are constantly growing, creating, and asking for more. Be self-compassionate as you navigate through it all. Trust that your experiences are paving the path to a bigger purpose. Every step of the way, remain confident in your abilities. Growth can bend you, stretch you, but it will never break you; it builds you. Believe that you are doing the best you can with where you are. Experiences either strengthen or reveal who you truly are. Struggle happens when you fight how it will all unfold in your life. Success occurs when you let go of the resistance and welcome the newly empowered you trying to emerge. Everything you need is already within you and will be unleashed right on time.

October 15

I am finding my happiness in the now.

Are you getting impatient because you need to see results before you believe you can create more? Or do you doubt your ability to get what you desire? It is easy to get discouraged when what you work for isn't materializing fast enough. Don't get distracted focusing on the goal and miss the greatness gained from the grind. Focus on what makes you happy while you wait on your miracles to manifest. Find the amazing things happening at every step of your journey and appreciate them. Divine timing is designed to teach you how to trust that everything is always working out for you. Remember, blessings are never delayed; you are the one that's rushing the manifestation.

October 16

I am creating my reality, and it is amazing.

Unresolved hurt only makes a heart heavy and hinders you from expanding to your fullest potential. Let it all go and find peace with where you have been, then decide where you want to go. Releasing and purging the pain is not about forgetting what happened. It is about accepting you cannot change your past, but you have the power to create your future. At some point, you have to let go of what you think should happen and live in what is truly happening. No one wants to face reality, especially when it's not what they want, but you will only find a way to move forward when you accept what is real. Use what you have and create the life you deserve. Looking back only slows you down from moving forward.

October 17

I am making my dreams my reality.

Appreciate your ability to create the experiences you want. Be willing to do the work necessary to improve what you want to change. You can't just have faith things will work out; you must also have faith in your ability to work them out. Show up and meet the Universe halfway by believing you have what it takes to manifest your dreams. Yes, the Universe has the power to bring all that you ask for, but you need to create the space for it to manifest. You are constantly deciding what you want your life to look like with your decisions. Be aware of all your choices and the opportunities they bring. If you don't learn to give all of you, you won't understand how to receive all you can create.

October 18

I am compassionate with myself.

Give yourself room to make mistakes and keep learning. Allow yourself the time you need to reorganize after a moment where things didn't work out. Show yourself compassion by resting, not quitting. Encourage yourself to keep going by celebrating the progress you are making in all areas of your life. Keep pursuing your dreams by getting back on the path. Don't forget to enjoy your wins. Happiness is found in the now. Life meets you where you elevate yourself to meet it. Showing up after a setback reflects that you embrace every step of the journey. Have faith things will continue to fall into place. Be open to learning, changing, and creating. Remember, you are constantly receiving what you asked for, and things are working out for you.

October 19

I am making great decisions with the life I am creating.

Every day is a new opportunity to create change. Remember, you are constantly being given two blessings - time and choices. Take control of how you use your choices by spending your time appreciating your life. You can choose to be happy with what you have or choose to focus on what you lack. Find your joy, spend your time being grateful for the amazing life you have, and make all your choices count. At this moment, you are worthy of everything you desire. You are always writing the story of your life, one decision at a time. Believe in your power of creation by being mindful of your choices. Enjoying where you are, prepares you for where you are going.

October 20

I am not far from what I desire.

Partial commitment does not make a full manifestation. Never wait to be happy; embrace every moment given to make your best life. Put as much effort into planting as you give to preparing and receiving. Remember, you are always attracting the resources you need to complete your vision. Your job is to focus on improving your mental, spiritual, and emotional well-being. The more you grow, the easier you will find the inspiration to keep climbing to the top. You will never doubt what you deserve when you believe in who you are. Trust the Universe is working behind the scenes to move you in the direction of your dreams. Only you can welcome your thriving. Your work on your well-being will be worth it. You're not far from what you desire. Stay the course.

October 21

I am building and believing in my blessings.

When you haven't developed your faith in yourself or the Universe to deliver, you become impatient. Don't block what you are building with doubt derived from your past; believe in the potential of your future. When you fully trust your request will manifest, timing becomes irrelevant. Have faith it will happen right on time. Be at peace with your past and direct your thoughts to focus on what's in front of you. Allow positive feelings to fuel your momentum forward. Optimistic outlooks create a commitment to building happiness. You are getting closer to receiving what you have been making, but the creating should not stop there. Keep asking for more.

October 22

I am trusting things are lining up for me.

Sometimes the lesson isn't about love; it's about the relationship with yourself. Sometimes the desire for more isn't about abundance; it's about removing your lack mindset. Sometimes the path isn't about finding peace; it's about developing your inner well-being. Whatever the challenge, you are the transformation. You can either stay stuck in the lesson or rise above to the victory. Remember, your happiness is your responsibility. No one is coming to save you. However, you can allow others to support you along the way. Trust that at this moment, things are lining up and working out for you. Never lose confidence in your ability to create the story you want to tell.

October 23

I am aligning my faith with my actions.

Having hope and faith are significant parts of the process of creation. Hope is the feeling that things will work out. Faith is a complete trust that things are working out. If you want to develop your resilience, add courage to face the facts, patience to find solutions, and discipline to continue despite the results. Remember, you are always on the way to creating the life you want. As long as you are living and growing, learning will never stop. Expansion is eternal. Your happiness requires lifelong commitment and effort. Life is about taking it one step and a day at a time. Don't get stuck trying to figure it all out at once. Relax, enjoy the journey and the process of creation.

October 24

I am fully committed to my happiness.

Look at your mistakes as an indicator of areas you can improve. Look at your loss as teachings on how to gain more. Look at your lows as opportunities to journey higher. Look at your blocks as redirection to your true path. When you realize your experiences are your preparation, the faster you get to your destination. Fighting any transformation will create unnecessary resistance. Stop pushing against the tides of your life; let go and go with the flow. When you surrender to a bigger purpose and not fixate on momentary needs, your thriving comes more easily. Trust it all leads to big rewards. At this moment, the Universe is conspiring with you for amazing things to happen.

October 25

I am on the right path to my success.

Your focus on the problem causes the struggle. Your attention to the solution will create your success. Happiness isn't discovered when you worry about what's going wrong; it is produced when you do more of what will make things right. You have what it takes to create change. Keep working through and pushing through until your breakthrough. Trust you are always moving forward, even if you feel stuck or stagnant. You are on the right path. Your progress can be improved habits, upgraded mindsets, knowing when to rest and not quit, or the discipline to keep going. Remember, where you are today is further than where you were yesterday. Keep showing up for yourself and your happiness.

October 26

I am working on my well-being.

Never be ashamed of the areas in your life that need improvement. Whether it's habits, mindsets, or self-worth that need work, remember to be kind to yourself as you keep trying. Be compassionate with your words as you learn and grow. Be patient as you pursue the path to more. Be committed as you focus on who you need to become to live the life you desire. No one is born with all the answers or their entire life vision. Keep setting boundaries, releasing dependencies, removing self-limiting thoughts, and welcoming your leveling up to more. If you put in the work, you will be reaping the rewards. Celebrate the great job you are doing to become the best version of yourself. Every effort you make will add up to big, beautiful blessings.

October 27

I am believing, preparing, and aligning with the happiness I seek.

Yes, sometimes the reality of your life can seem unfair, but it is up to you to face it, resolve it, and move forward. Remember, you cannot only rely on faith; you must add belief in your ability to create a way out. Start with the understanding that everything is always working out for you then act to create change. Persistence and preparation will bring the results you seek. Today, show up and courageously meet life where it is trying to meet you. You will thrive through this. Focus on what you can control and allow it to guide you to solutions. Be proud of who you are and what you are creating. You deserve it all.

October 28

I am always moving forward.

When you want something, don't contradict it with disbelief. You attract abundance by believing you already have everything you need to create it. You can attract love by reconnecting with what makes you feel worthy. You can attract miracles by trusting in all that you deserve. Live with confidence that your victory is already done and everything you desire is already on its way to you. Move past 'asking' for what you need and start 'thanking' for its delivery. Put power into your thoughts and actions and keep creating the change you want in your life. You can find your joy by celebrating now and not waiting until when things fall into place. Whatever you need, remember you already have it within. Keep expressing gratitude for the unfolding success in your life. Your miracles are done.

October 29

I am aligning with the fullness of who I am.

The Universe is always giving you feedback. When you are not aligned with what your soul needs to thrive, an imbalance of emotions will prevail. Don't discard them; welcome them because they are signaling you to what must be changed. Consider negative feelings as a guidance system steering you towards what you need to move forward. Use emotions like gratitude to guide you back to a place of peace, happiness, healing, and balance. The better you feel, the more you create. The more you create, the more you are confident in what you can manifest. Remember, you are capable of producing your plenty. Tune in to the fullness of who you are to keep you moving forward.

October 30

I am manifesting more than I can imagine.

Between the moment you ask and the moment your request manifests, time is needed for things to fall into place. Don't use the opportunity to doubt. Use it wisely by adding more details to your dreams. Consider the 'waiting' an opportunity to keep moving forward by asking for more. In every moment, you are gaining momentum toward a vision far beyond what you initially requested. Believe things are working in your favor even before you know how they will unfold. Trust the process that is trying to get you to where you want to go. Your paths are being cleared, bridges are being built, and your rewards are constantly being prepared. Creation never stops; you shouldn't either.

October 31

I am attracting greatness because I am grateful.

Always believe that everything is working out for you. When you think that things are falling apart, understand they are miraculously falling into place. Sometimes foundations must break before you can rebuild and become the best version of yourself. Life will upgrade and transform you for your promise of abundance and purpose. You can find your best self today. It is the part of you that is always in harmony with who you truly are. Remember, you have the power to design the day you want. When you find peace with where you are, you uncover the inspiration and strength to move forward. Today is your day! Purpose attracts possibilities, and gratitude attracts greatness.

November 01

I am always loved.

This November, I am centering myself with Divine grace and gratitude for my blessings. I am releasing the thoughts that do not serve my happiness. I am welcoming the pouring of prosperity and well-being into my life. I am faith-full that everything is working out for me. I am proud of the progress I am making with my life. I am grateful for the transforming mindset that is helping me pursue the success and happiness I desire. My growth inspires me. My focus encourages me to create more. I am moving past what has gone, I appreciate what remains, and I am looking forward to what's to come. Thank you, Source, for protecting, supporting, providing for, and loving me always. My heart and soul are at peace because I trust life is on my side.

November 02

I am destined to be victorious.

Remember, nothing happens ahead of its time. Wherever you think you are on your journey, have faith you are moving forward. You are constantly expanding and creating new wants and desires. How else would you progress if you don't develop more preferences? You won't know what you possess until who you are is questioned. You won't know what you can endure until the pressure is applied. You won't know what courage you can muster until you have been under fire. You won't know up until you have been down. The experiences you face were designed to uncover the real you. Stay focused, and don't allow timing to distract you from staying on the course to your more. Keep going.

November 03

I am investing in my future.

Time cannot be saved for future use, but you can be wise and invest it in the future you. What you do today creates your tomorrow. You cannot only wish for what you want; you must put in the mental, emotional, and spiritual work to make it materialize. Hopes and dreams always start as a seed and aren't immediately fruitful. Remember seeds take time, nurturing, love, and effort to grow. Getting impatient will not make them flourish any faster. What is for you always shows up at the right time. Keep trusting that your planting is consistently producing, even when you do not see the progress. Give your seed time to push through the dirt. Keep believing and trusting you have what it takes to create your all. Before you know it, your fruit will blossom.

November 04

I am growing in my greatness.

Start your day not reliving the past but by defining how you show up for yourself in the present. Holding on to the old version of yourself only blocks the blessings of the improved you that's trying to emerge. Your transformation is unavoidable. Who you are at this moment is always more than who you were yesterday. Find reasons to course-correct rather than complain. One of your biggest blessings is the opportunity every morning to make a change in how you create. Only you can transmute the bitter from the past and build better for your future. You have plenty to be thankful for; take the time to look and appreciate where you are. When you count your blessings, life will reward you with more. Remember, you are deserving of all good things.

November 05

I am preparing for my plenty.

Your life will change when you focus on what you have gained, not what you have lost. It is human nature to see what is missing rather than what is manifesting. Life wants you to win. It will pour blessings slowly to teach you how to prepare for your plenty. Learn to manage what you have before you can thrive with what you have asked for receiving. Start where you are standing because movement requires momentum. Yes, the journey thus far may not have been the smoothest. No, you are not failing; you are learning. Yes, you feel tired and doubtful of your ability to move forward. No, you cannot quit, but you can rest. Use your time to mentally prepare for the new levels you are about to attain. You are not where you are by chance; use your choices to get you higher.

November 06

I am Divinely supported.

Let go of who you were yesterday, embrace who you are today, and build on who you want to be tomorrow. Do not define your now by your circumstances but by your unlimited possibilities. You have what it takes to empower yourself and claim your right to build the life you desire. Align with your true self by trusting you always have what you need to succeed. Today choose to be contented with your life and find something to appreciate. No matter what you face, believe you are always Divinely loved and supported. Forget the trials of yesterday and focus on the triumphs of today. Yes, the past made you question your ability to create your win, but there is always something in the present to show you that you are worthy of more.

November 07

I am making every moment count.

Doubt can kill more dreams than failure ever will. Failure teaches, but doubt will prevent you from doing what is needed to create the life you want. Don't let worrying about results rob you of the time required to create change in the now. Everything takes time to manifest and begins with the belief that you deserve it. Find a reason that defeats doubt, and nothing will hold you back. Instead of fear, express gratitude, and refocus. Understand there is always a reason for the season and a purpose to the pace. Don't allow time to make you give up on your dreams. The Universe is ALL ways working things out in your favor. Make today count.

November 8

I am trusting more opportunities are available.

When you work on who you are, you progress faster along your path. Focus on who you need to be, and you will get where you want to go. Say thank you to every door you knocked on that didn't open. Rejoice that it stopped you from getting into places and situations where you did not belong. A closed door is designed to help you discover your destiny. What is meant for you will always open and welcome you. Trust that more opportunities are available. Your way through will always be cleared ahead of you. Do the work to develop healthy daily habits, and you will be unstoppable. Blocked paths can be blessings to beautiful beginnings.

November 09

I am being spontaneously blessed.

Worrying delays your satisfaction. The time you spend worrying prevents you from doing the work needed to get things resolved. When you stop doubting when your prayers will be answered, the Universe will begin to surprise you with new opportunities, fated occurrences, and surprising coincidences. Let go of how you think your blessings should arrive and allow yourself to be amazed by life's generosity. Pay attention to the goodness happening now. What is meant for you will come to you. There is no need to go out and effort for it. Be patient and trust in Divine timing. The elements are always working in your favor. Before you know it, all you want will materialize.

November 10

I am celebrating who I am becoming.

Unworthiness is a lie you tell yourself when you feel your dreams are unattainable. Every single person was born with the ability to create the life they desire. Remember, you deserve all the happiness you can imagine. Today reflect on what you have gone through, not to live in the past, but to honor your progress and keep trusting the process. You have learned and created from your loss. You have become stronger and stuck to the pursuit of your happiness. You have made sure you do not repeat old habits trying to get new results. You have worked diligently to improve yourself and your situation. Be grateful and celebrate who you are becoming. You were born worthy of all.

November 11

I am creating what I am worthy of.

When you ignore your blessings and focus on the lack, you develop anxiety and stress about what's not going your way. Don't let the deficiency distract you; trust it was sent to guide you to more. You are in control of where your attention goes and what cultivates. How you respond to what you don't want, welcomes what you do want. It all begins with believing that you do not have to be anyone or do anything to prove your worthiness. Worthiness is your birthright. Only you can pursue the highest vision for your life. The Universe will help you create it all the moment you decide to go for it all. Stop worrying. Start believing in the abundance you want to welcome.

November 12

I am acknowledging the blessings in my life.

Progress can be big external validations or small mindset shifts that lead to the abundance you want. The most important part of change is who you become. Your relationship with yourself is the most significant influence on what is possible in your life. Don't miss out on your miracles because you are not committed to connecting with your best self. Bring all of you and use it to build a full life. Show up for your happiness by working today for what you want tomorrow. Take a moment to stop and acknowledge the blessings already building around you. Truly see the miracles manifesting. Bask in the sunshine and appreciate the storm you just passed through. Life is good.

November 13

I am aligning and thriving.

Today let your thoughts focus on alignment with what makes your soul flourish. Slow down enough to reconnect with yourself, your well-being, and the status of your dreams. Checking in helps you uncover any mental, emotional, and spiritual needs that aren't being met. Explore how you are feeling and how you want to feel. Celebrate how well you are doing with your happiness. You are the only one that can recognize the wholeness of your heart. You are the only one that can master the mindset that creates your happiness. You are the only one that can plant the seeds that blossom into abundance. You are the only one that can pursue the life you desire. You are the only one that can show up and shine. Remember, everything you need is already within you. Align and thrive.

November 14

I am worthy of having all.

When you doubt what you deserve, what you want does not show up when you expect. Asking from lack will limit what you can create. The Universe is ready and waiting to give you what you requested. After you prayed for something, you are transformed into who you need to be to receive it. That process can take some time, and you determine the length of it. Do your part to reduce the wait, release your resistance to the change. What is meant for you will never miss you, and what is sent to you is intended to teach and create a new you. Let go of what you think you should have already gained, and look at what you have actually achieved. Meet life where it is trying to meet you. You are worthy of having it all. Become the person who trusts in their possibilities.

November 15

I am unstoppable.

You empower yourself when you create a breakthrough from a breakdown. Don't stay stuck, believe at this moment, you are being Divinely pushed, pulled, and carried to more. Pushed to find your healing after hurt. Pulled forward to a purpose-driven life. Carried to abundant blessings and miracles you never thought were possible. Only you can discover what you deserve. Use self-compassion while you release the mindset that is holding you back from reconnecting with your full potential. Appreciating what you have does not mean you don't want to have more; it means you understand that you can create more. Learn to love your life during your leveling up. What you have now is enough to build the next. Knowing your worth makes you unstoppable

November 16

I am obsessively grateful.

When you pray, you are always given something to create what you want. Wherever you think you are in life, make the best of it. Do not disregard what you have; it is essential to the creation of more. Always see the benefit of the small because it creates the potential for all. Focus on your blessings; they are all around you in different stages of manifestation. Be obsessive about expressing your gratitude for where you are and what you desire. There is nothing wrong with wanting more, which is separate from being thankful for what you have. Remember, it is not always about counting your blessings; it's about activating the positive emotion of gratitude. Positive feelings enhance creativity and your potential for attracting more.

November 17

I am proud of my progress.

Most people wait until they've achieved their goals to be proud of themselves. Finding moments to appreciate your progress will keep you moving forward. Don't limit yourself by reserving your happiness for the destination. You live a fulfilled life when you focus on your joy throughout your journey. Today applaud what you are doing to change your life. Keep focusing on the unlimited possibilities available to you. Be grateful for the abundance of goodness in simple things. Open yourself to a new attitude of gratitude, prosperity, and joy. Trust that all is well and move forward with a renewed sense of assurance. You are the one making all the effort to achieve every single win you experience. Why are you delaying your delight? Celebrate now, not 'when.'

November 18

I am inspired to keep going for more.

People who attach their happiness to outcomes never experience true satisfaction. Every major achievement has smaller parts that make up the whole. Don't miss the beauty in the unfolding because you are distracted by the goal. A full manifestation is not necessary for happiness. You have to make creating enough. As long as you are alive, you will have desires. Every day is a new blessing and opportunity to experience our magnificent, abundant world. Be amazed at what you have conquered and what you will accomplish. See the beauty in the process of becoming the best version of yourself. When you focus on your progress, you inspire yourself to keep going after more. Your true goal should be joy.

November 19

I am encouraged by my growth.

Learning to embrace change will make your transition into your life seasons better. Understand the setbacks are only sent to help you define what you want when you step up. When you are forced to step back, it is setting you up to make leaps forward. Trust that every up, down, back, and forth has the purpose of moving you to the right place at the right time. Just like you have to prepare for where you are going, the pieces need time to fall into place for when you get there. Seasons have reasons, and they are all necessary to your journey. You are always blessed; it is with gratitude you recognize this. Whatever stage you are in, know you have what it takes to get through it all. You will get to the win. Life is a continuous cycle that is designed to encourage your growth. You've got this.

November 20

I am succeeding in all of my seasons.

Right before the manifestation of your dreams, you will know it. This is when fatigue creeps in and convinces you that you can't climb anymore. Rest, then go again. Everything unfolds right on time. Don't let anything stop you from continuing your journey. Celebrate your courage because you stepped up despite not knowing if you would level up. Acknowledge the blind faith it takes to keep going despite what you see. Remember, you cannot mess up your destiny. Be proud of yourself and your efforts. Before you move forward in faith, appreciate all that you are doing to create your life. Make your next step significant. Trust you are not about to fall; you are about to fly higher.

November 21

I am dedicated to my victory.

You have to put in the work if you want to win. Don't stay stuck because you lack confidence in your ability to produce your success. Your miracle may be one act of forgiveness away, one deliberate step away, one new habit away, one yes or no away. Your 'work' doesn’t have to be physical; it can be mental. Only you can decide what you need to develop your dedication and courage to go for the victory. Pay attention; there are always blessings manifesting for you daily. You have been supported, provided for, and protected from circumstances you could not imagine. Embrace today's opportunities to pursue the most significant vision you can dream for your life. Trust you have what it takes. You can create your happiness.

November 22

I am capable of creating my solutions.

Today pray for the grace and dignity you need to release what holds you back from finding what makes your heart full and your Soul be at peace. Remember, only your beliefs have limits. Take the time to identify, acknowledge, and release yours. You have what it takes to move past this moment to more abundant times. You are enough, and you are doing the best you can. Trust your ability to focus on how you can create more. You are skilled and very capable of finding your solutions. Make self-compassion essential to your thriving. You are destined for a life full of plentiful possibilities. Get ready to receive all that you are working on manifesting.

November 23

I am patient with my process.

The need to control how life should unfold is where disappointment can set in. When you think you are blocked, trust you are being saved from things you cannot see. Your view to the top can be limited by where you are standing. What's preventing you from moving up is only there to redirect your focus to the best path. You are shaped by every challenge you conquered because you stayed committed to the course. Strong foundations aren't created by chance; they are built when you use your experiences to transform your life. Let a higher purpose guide you there. When you ask for a better life, you cannot take it back. Go with the flow. Allow your dreams to manifest in ways you could not have imagined. Be patient with the process that guides you to the top.

November 24

I am priceless and worthy of all.

Don't let the fear of losing affection or recognition keep you from expressing who you are. No matter what you do, believe that the value you bring is always the same. Others should never define the significance of what you have to offer. Never discount your time, love, abilities, or talents because of how anyone reacts to them. Believe in your worth first, then set appropriate boundaries. Stop holding on to what you cannot control and focus on what you can - YOU. Don't let anyone make you doubt your destiny. Concentrate on your happiness; you are worthy. Your life vision is your own and no one else's. Life is constantly pushing you toward your dreams. When you stay the course, the right circumstances and people will show up to match your value.

November 25

I am prepared to prosper.

Everyone has a dream they are working on manifesting. Create the fruitful future you want with three principles: vision, intent, and inspired action. Vision because you must know where you are going before the way is revealed to you. Intent because you have to find emotional clarity and believe in your vision before you go. Inspired action because you must first work on who you need to be, then be Divinely guided there. Your experiences will teach you how to let go of the limiting version to pursue the highest vision for your life. Get clear, concentrate on feeling good, and prepare to prosper. Remember, you don't have to fight to keep what's yours, and what's yours will always find a way to get to you. Focus on the future you want. Trust the path is already made.

November 26

I am trusting I always have what I need.

It takes courage, commitment, and consistency to pursue your peace after pain. Yes, making that first move toward creating anything better can be challenging, but it is necessary. It is a natural response to see healing as a challenge. However, life will not change until you change. Believe you will grow stronger with every step you take. Nothing substantial is built in a day, and your transformation will not happen overnight. Don't overwhelm yourself. You can grow slowly. When your doubt gets loud, quiet it with self-compassion. Trust you already have what it takes to succeed. Don't take your old baggage on your new journey. Healing is essential to your happiness.

November 27

I am creating positive thoughts, new habits, and better beliefs.

Consider every morning you wake up a new opportunity to start over, stronger and wiser than before. Don't let past experiences keep you stuck and doubting your abilities. Instead, leave yesterday where it is. Appreciate today and begin with optimistic thoughts, improved habits, and better beliefs. Reclaim your happiness. Be thankful for the opportunity to work on manifesting more. How blessed are you to be given another chance to create what you want? Remember, you cannot mess up what is meant to be. You cannot lose what is yours. You cannot get life wrong; you can only learn along the way how to make it right. Trust it is all working out for your highest good. All you can do is your best and show up. Every effort counts.

November 28

I am amazed at my growth.

Today, set aside the distraction from your challenges and focus on your growth. Don't let your pace to win the race keep you from seeing your progress. You walked miles without realizing the importance of the steps you were taking. You succeeded because you took chances with small probabilities of winning. Marvel at how much you have grown in all areas of your life. Be grateful for the distance you have reached and the hurdles your discernment helped you avoid. Sometimes you get distracted by what you lack and never consider what you were saved from. There is so much the Universe is doing to protect you. Use gratitude to keep you grounded. Keep going; you are crushing it. Your miracle is in your transformation.

November 29

I am faithful my doors are already opened.

Trust you are never facing difficulties alone. You are always Divinely supported through the experiences that redefine how you consider your worthiness for happiness. Everything is working in your favor, even when you do not see it. How else would you get clear on what you want if you don't cleanse what holds you back from going further? At this moment, the Universe is working for you, with you, and ahead of you. Have faith that your doors are already opened. They are waiting on you to confidently walk through them. Stay thankful, focused, and keep pushing forward to better. You are blessed. You are deserving of all good things. Remember how worthy you are.

November 30

I am honoring my happiness.

Figure out what you want before you proceed. Trying to create from uncertainty will only make you doubt your ability to complete what you started. Don't try to run when you need to rest; this will make you question the quality of your steps. Take a deep breath, tune in to how you want to feel, and let it guide you forward. Before you move forward, acknowledge the positive transformations that can come from slowing down. You can learn to listen more attentively to what your soul wants. You can use compassion to repair and restore important relationships. You can create more clarity with what you want for your life. Sometimes the ability to rest gets you ready for when you get your go. Honoring your happiness builds your confidence.

December 01

I am moving in the right direction.

This month I am aligning with the best of who I am. I am concentrating on solutions and releasing my need to overthink. I am improving my confidence in my ability to overcome what holds me back. I am progressing with my faith and pushing past my fears. I am attracting the resources I need to help me thrive. I am welcoming cleared paths to the direction of my happiness. I am committed to becoming who I need to be to live the highest vision of my life. As I continue to fulfill my purpose, I am Divinely guided, supported, protected, provided for, and loved. Thank you, Universe, for always steering me toward the best life has to offer me. I am blessed.

December 02

I am always being blessed with better.

Whatever you may be experiencing, keep focusing on your blessings, not the timing. Don't allow delays to distract you from the progress you are making. No matter what you face, you have to believe in a better future. Find your confidence by remembering that challenges are always conquered, and miracles always manifest. You were not Divinely guided this far to be forgotten about right before the win. Believe in the abundant goodness that is destined for you. There is a change about to happen; trust you are ready for it. You have prepared enough, and a breakthrough is at the breaking point. Surrender to the timing by letting the worry go. Stay faith FULL, my friend.

December 03

I am making progress, and I am succeeding.

Express your gratitude today for your progress. Move past asking for more and start thanking for what you already have and what is yet to come. Keep expressing appreciation for the love, happiness, and abundance that surrounds you. Many things have manifested for you; acknowledge and celebrate them. Pray with confidence what you are working on is already yours. Pray with faith you are prepared to receive big blessings at a moment's notice. Pray with positive expectation that things are continuing to work out for you. Keep standing firm in an attitude of gratitude. Remember also to be proud of yourself. You are doing a great job with your happiness. You are abundantly blessed.

December 04

I am giving my soul what it needs to thrive.

The most rewarding relationship you can develop is the one with yourself. Practicing happiness will keep you motivated as you work on more. Finding what makes you smile will help you acknowledge how good life is to you. Exploring what sets you apart will help you make the abundance you want to see manifest. Connecting with what inspires you to create will motivate you to keep building a better life. Seeing what magnifies your inner beauty will push you to amplify the best of who you are. Get to know who you are by focusing on how you want to feel and let that fuel your unlimited possibilities. Take the time to know yourself. Give your beautiful soul what it needs to shine through it all.

December 05

I am pursuing my all.

Don't discard the fight to survive; it created your passion for thriving. Bless the struggle you endured; it activated your pursuit of success. Thank the constant pushing forward; it uncovered your strength. Forgive the rejection you received; it revealed your true worth through self-acceptance. Embrace the desire you developed for more; it ignited your fire to pursue your all. Every season had a reason and shaped you into the person ready for the abundant blessings coming your way. You cannot fully understand who you are without accepting what shaped you. Be grateful for your expanding possibilities. Your life has been a beautiful story filled with miracles. Embrace all of you; it created more of you.

December 06

I have faith I will be fruitful.

Consider your ideas your seeds. Plant them and be confident that what you are growing will eventually start budding. Move past the worrying about if, when, or how the transformation will happen. Instead, have faith everything is leading to your flourishing. Yes, occasionally, you may have to push through the dirt to see the sunshine, but trust that the Universe has given you everything you need to thrive. The more ideas you plant, the further along your path you progress. Remember, you are never pushed into a position without the provision to get what's promised. All your ideas will eventually grow into a beautiful life vision. Keep dreaming, planting, and expecting an abundant harvest. Be patient as it all becomes more. Have faith; you will be fruitful.

December 07

I am improving my relationship with myself.

If you feel unloved, pay attention to your self-love and self-care routine. If you are distracted by lack, work on your abundance mindset. If you feel lost, find your direction by connecting with your inner wisdom. Whatever is holding you back, conquer it by improving your relationship with it. Feeling stuck is a sign that something in your life requires attention and improvement. Face it and move forward to where you want to go. Face it and get back to creating bigger. Face it because you know you deserve to have better. Face it because you want to keep building the life you envision. Face it because you are destined to become more. When you face the challenge, the change you desire will follow.

December 08

I am focused forward.

Disappointment happens when you let your desire for manifestations overshadow your need to feel happy at this moment. Yes, you want your dreams to materialize, but how you feel before it arrives is very important. Life is always working to give you what you need, learn to relax, and allow it to come to you. Remember, you are the point of attraction. Your work is to become the right environment for what you desire. What is meant for you will never miss you, and what is sent to you is intended to teach and create a new you. Let go of what you think you should have gained and look at what you did achieve. Don't let the disappointment of where you are, keep distracting you from where you are going.

December 09

I am kind and compassionate with myself.

No one said life would be easy, or there wouldn't be any struggle to stay focused. You will get tired, overwhelmed, or feel uncertain. If you are weary, rest and recoup. If you feel stuck, sit, listen inward, then regain your footing. If you are overwhelmed, take a deep breath, slow down, then go. Remember, you are human, and you need to fine-tune your well-being occasionally. Don't judge yourself for having feelings, be okay with them; they signal that something needs attention. Instead, learn to understand your emotions and discern your responses to them. No one is ever 100 percent in 'go' mode. Honor how you feel and give yourself compassion to get through it all.

December 10

I am deserving of all good things.

Yes, it is normal to feel disheartened about life from time to time, but that does not mean happiness is not possible to regain. Yes, it is normal to feel lost, but that does not mean you should give up on your dreams. Yes, it is normal to feel uncertain about what to do, but that does not mean you should not keep moving forward. You don't always have to know how to go, where you go, or where to start; just go. You don't have to be perfect; just keep trying your best. Remember, you are unique, creative, amazing, lovable, and remarkable. Don't let anything you experience take the belief of who you are from your heart. Trust you are very capable of creating more. Keep doing the best you can with where you are. You, my friend, have the power to change your life.

December 11

I am thanking for my ability to welcome more.

Today is a perfect day to believe in all of your dreams. It is also a great day to embrace the abundant possibilities that life has to offer you. Trust your plan to create more is supported, and your path is cleared ahead of you. You already have the provisions you need to find fulfillment on your journey to your purpose. Your abundance is already prepared. Your genuine connections are already aligned. Your success is already showing up. Trust what you want is already done. Remember, from the moment you ask, and when your desire manifests, there is a gap in time. Use it to master the skills and patience to create more. Always enjoy the life you are building.

December 12

I am nurturing my blessings, and they are blossoming.

Everything you need to create the life you want is already within you. The most important thing you can do along the way is to develop a relationship with yourself. Trust every aspect of your journey is necessary. Every step helps to reveal what you know about who you are. When you know what you are capable of creating, nothing keeps you from having it all. The continuous need to create and reevaluate your dreams is what life is about. Some changes have you standing by before the step up. Some challenges have you building your strength to build significant blessings. Changes and challenges are what you need to learn to walk until it works. Every season has a reason for your progress.

December 13

I am focused on my happiness.

Remember, another person's healing will not improve your life or change your past. You are the one that must be consistent with making your happiness happen. Start with connecting with your true self, and you will understand your real power. Work on your ability to create solutions, and you will find your way. Practice forgiveness, and you will find your emotional freedom. Believe in your worth, your efforts, and your possibilities. Trust you are doing the best you can with what you know. Change your doubt into doing more. Do what you need to get done to build the life you want. Do what's best for your emotional well-being. Do more of what feels good to you. Let today be a day of positive transformation. Trust you have what it takes to create the change you desire.

December 14

I am steadfastly working on my potential to prosper.

If you are steadfast in your work, your wishes will manifest. Despite the storms, do not abandon ship; take control, and ride it out. Don't quit because answers aren't coming as quickly as you want. Blessings always manifest right after the moment you want to stop. Remember, life is always preparing you to build more than you had before. The storm will be over soon, and you won't remember how you made it through or how you managed to survive. The experience will bring the lessons that cleanse as well as nourish. What you create after it all is up to you. Trust you won't be the same person who walked in, but someone better—someone who truly understands their potential to prosper.

December 15

I am Divinely steered toward the best life has to offer.

Being mindful of what you think will help you better create what you want. For the thoughts that don't support your progress, remember you have the power to rephrase them more positively. When unwanted thoughts show up, take a deep breath, then start over. Refocus on how you are able, not how you are unable because of your past. Only you can dismiss the distraction of doubt and allow thoughts that encourage you to work on solutions. Remember, a belief is a thought you continue to think; it can always be changed. New life stages require new thinking. The moment you begin to see yourself as worthy of what you work for is the instant you allow more of what you desire into your life.

December 16

I am stepping forward to my blessings.

When you have been through a season of struggle and stillness, believe the next natural stage is movement. Have faith that what you experience today will change tomorrow if you do the work. Keep moving, climbing, creating, trusting, and welcoming your blessings. Today, if you feel discouraged, ask for Divine support. Welcome the ability to overcome what holds you back. Invite the courage to see past this moment and believe in a better future. Ask for the fortitude to push beyond your doubt. Allow the inspired action to create more. Find patience with the pace. Be thankful for the strength to continue believing and knowing all will be well. Don't give up before your miracle manifests.

December 17

I am welcoming the peace and prosperity I pray for.

You improve your well-being when you improve your beliefs about your wholeness. Everything you want to transform begins with you. As you start to connect with the real you, you learn to overcome the thoughts or actions that hold you back. Remember, when you asked for a better life, it is given. Use what is created within you to create a new you. Don't forfeit your blessings because you are afraid to manage your setbacks. When life sends a challenge, don't get stuck, push forward, and take control with your responses. Look at your past achievements for assurance that you have what it takes to step over the struggle and step into success. Believe you are worthy and welcome your prosperity.

December 18

I am on a mission of guaranteed success.

Blocks are blessings in disguise. Any door that closed on you was never yours to enter. You were being redirected to better opportunities. Obstacles turn you in the direction of where you are supposed to go. Look beyond where you think you are and acknowledge the other possibilities being made available. What is yours cannot be denied or delayed. Remember, there is always more. See yourself on a mission of guaranteed success and change what you pray for. Understand that what you need most to ensure the win is commitment and the ability to overcome the obstacles in your way. Once you master your mental might, you push through anything.

December 19

I am trusting my prosperity is already prepared.

If you feel challenged, remember, nothing remains the same forever. Have faith things will improve. Trust the trying and triumphant times both have a purpose. To transform your thoughts towards more positivity, find something in your life to appreciate. The more grateful you are, the more you acknowledge that you have what you need in every moment. You are moved into a position of promise when you are ready. Everything you go through teaches you the principles you need to prosper. Learn to manage the down before the up, the little before the plenty, and the rejection before affection. What you don't want is there to help you define what you do want.

December 20

I am thankful for my blessings.

There is a difference between being faithful to your plan and faith-full to the plan for your life. When you are too faithful to your plan, you may not recognize when to let go or change course. When you are full of faith, you understand that what is for you will always come to you. When you put purpose into your day, nothing can hold you back from accomplishing your goals. You begin to understand the reasons for the seasons and refuse to give up on your dreams. Today refocus and express gratitude for your valleys and mountaintops. Before you can earn the right to be thankful up top, you must be thankful down below. Stay faith-full and trust that all things, at all times, are working out in your favor. Right now, you have everything you need to thrive.

December 21

I am skilled enough to create the success I desire.

Change is feared when you don't trust your abilities. Believe you can create the happiness you want. Success begins when you understand you are equipped with what you need. Do you think you went through all that struggle and strengthening for nothing? Don't be distracted by what you did not get; focus on the skills you learned and commit to crushing your goals. Today step back a bit to regroup and figure out what you need. Sometimes you need to stop, recharge, then return wiser and clear with a solid plan to manifest your dreams. There is a difference between giving up and taking a rest. Take time to regain your footing, then step forward.

December 22

I am born to create.

You are a creator born to create. Take ownership of your dreams. Only you can bring them into reality the way you want them. Trust that Divine forces are working behind the scenes to help make them your reality. Remember, you are never given a vision without the provision to make it prosper. Opportunities to move forward are opening up for you. Hold trust that more than you can imagine possible will manifest soon. Today, if you have been praying for answers, we encourage you to be open to how you receive them. Source responds in a variety of ways and is always giving you feedback. The repetitive numbers, thoughts, feelings, and ideas that keep showing up are guiding you to the solutions you seek. Pay attention. You are constantly being directed to your highest good.

December 23

I am pushing forward to my victory.

Stop complaining about what you go through and start 'thanking' for them. Thank every closed door because they directed you to your opened door. Being good does not always mean you get good, but you will learn what is good for you. Resist thinking about what you should have done better, how you should have been better, or why you didn't make better choices. Today move past old situations and stop looking back. It is all behind you now. Look forward and declare you will triumph despite the past. Embrace your power to create right now. Focus on how you want to feel and let it influence what you are doing. Your better will manifest.

December 24

I am going for it all.

Creation requires commitment and won't manifest without work. Yes, taking the first step to making the life you want comes with a bit of discomfort, but nothing will happen unless you go for it. Don't stay small because you doubt your abilities. Go big, brave, and bold, and show the world your capabilities. If you don't bet on yourself, no one else will. Today take a moment to find your sense of balance between your peace and your strength. Use this time to focus on the light on your face and leave the darkness behind you. Do not underestimate the power you can produce from the pain you have pushed past. Friction and focus create fire! Light the fire within by working on who you are. Stop waiting for a light at the end of the tunnel. Remember, you are the light.

December 25

I am trusting the path to my plenty.

Learn to appreciate your lessons, not resist them. Everything you survived has prepared you for your purpose and is valuable to your happiness. Trials and triumph teach you what is important and who is important. How else would you know who has your back? You may lose people along the way, but never your purpose. Never let the lesson win. Combat challenging feelings with positive affirmations. Repeat them as many times as you need to and conquer the doubt by doing more. Start with believing you are worthy, and you have the power to overcome anything. Trust in your path. What's in you is always stronger than what's happening around you. Focus.

December 26

I am grateful for the miracles manifesting in my life.

Some things come easy, and others require more effort. Don't get distracted with the work and ignore what you already have. There is happiness around you; appreciate it no matter the form of delivery. Being grateful for your existing blessings will welcome more miracles manifesting. Give yourself some peace-filled space by setting an intention to bring your awareness into your here and now. Well-being begins with focusing on how you want to feel in every moment. Release the worry. Do the best you can with whatever comes your way. Let tomorrow happen tomorrow. Let today unfold as it should. Everything will work out for you right on time. Trust all your efforts are paying off.

December 27

I am Divinely supported, protected, and loved.

When you stop reliving the past, you define how you show up for yourself in the present. Holding on to the old version of yourself only blocks the blessings of the improved you that's trying to emerge. Who you are at this moment is always more than who you were before. Your transformation is unavoidable. You are constantly expanding and creating new wants and desires. Life is always directing you to where you need to go to accomplish your purpose. The journey becomes a struggle when you fight against the flow. Let go of the control you think you need to win and welcome the guidance. Remember, you are always Divinely supported, protected, and loved.

December 28

I am abundantly blessed.

This is a reminder that you have created amazing things in your life before; right now, is no exception. Have patience today, my friend. What you are working on manifesting is already here. Slow down long enough to realize that it has already become your reality. Continue to stay strong, show up, and embrace your powers of creation. Only you can produce the abundant blessings you want to manifest for your future. Your experiences are meant to have you question the purpose of your life and push you toward the right path. Believe you are already supported and trust you have what you need to succeed constantly. Happiness is not when everything falls into place; it recognizes the miracles of them falling into place. See that you are already abundantly blessed.

December 29

I am always winning.

With grace and gratitude, allow life to remove what does not serve your happiness. Remember, clearing and creation require time and commitment. Today, welcome what helps you heal and reminds you that you are already whole. Stay patient throughout the transitions. All your experiences have been preparing you for your current lessons. Every past triumph and trial have equipped you for this very moment. Remember, you never lose; you only learn who you are. That makes you a winner. Move past your current situation with grace and call on the strength you have developed within. The reward will be more significant than you could even imagine, and the result will appear faster than you can perceive. Never fight change; embrace it.

December 30

I am a master mind.

The Universe is sending you healing and transformation as we speak. What you think you lack is a lesson in planting and patience. You must know how to live without, to understand living with. Lack is a lesson on learning the importance of living with gratitude. How else will you appreciate the abundance and the beauty of your harvest? Understand the power of your mind and program it for success. Get up, show up, and set the tone for how you want your day to go. When you expect good things, you allow great things. Know that you are always in control of your reactions and choices. Don't let the world take what you believe you are capable of building from you. Today be your mastermind. You are in control of what you create.

December 31

I am ready for the next and best.

As the year transitions, remember the improvements you made, the mindsets you changed, and the mountains you conquered to stand at the top. Yes, there were some twists, but celebrate the many gains after the turns. Give yourself credit for taking control of your responses, choices, and creations. Be grateful for the progress you have made despite what was experienced. Look forward to where you are going and be proud of who you are becoming. You are doing a great job with your well-being. Continue to be accepting and appreciative of the abundance constantly flowing to you. Bless this past year, and expect unlimited possibilities for the next. Trust you are stepping into a beautiful chapter full of significant blessings. You are worthy of all your dreams.

Cheers to a job well done!

You have completed months of a fantastic journey. We hope these Reminders for life helped you create more of what you desire. Great job on pushing forward, persevering, and making your happiness a priority. Today celebrate your victory and the incredible change you have created in your life from your routine of self-affirming actions. We invite you to check out more of our books and Journals.

Visit us at: www.ShopCommandingLife.com

Made in United States
North Haven, CT
05 May 2022